UNIVERSITY LIBRARY
UW - STEVENS

D0940611

The Make-or-Buy Decision

by

Anthony J. Gambino
Director of Accounting Standards
American Insurance Association

A study carried out on behalf of the
National Association of Accountants
New York, N.Y.
and
The Society of Management Accountants of Canada
Hamilton, Ontario, Canada

Published by

National Association of Accountants

919 Third Avenue, New York, N.Y. 10022

and

The Society of Management Accountants of Canada

154 Main St. E., Hamilton, Ontario, Canada

Copyright by National Association of Accountants © 1980
Copyright in Canada by The Society of Management Accountants of Canada © 1980
NAA Publication Number 80120
ISBN 0-86641-000-7

HD
30.23
.G35

Foreword

It is often feasible for a manufacturing firm to decide whether to make or to buy certain products or components for its production process. This alternative is present not only in the planning of a new product line, but also in the subsequent course of operations. The initial conditions may change and the firm might find it advantageous to switch from making to buying or vice versa. It is this kind of managerial thinking that constitutes the make-buy decision process.

The make-buy decision process involves a host of sensitive and complex considerations which are both financial and nonfinancial in nature. In other words, most of the relevant factors lend themselves to a quantitative analysis while some do not.

This report presents the findings of a research study which was designed to explore make-buy decisions as they are currently being made in business enterprises. The emphasis was, of course, on the analytical tools and their use, especially those that are or could be derived from the firm's management accounting information.

The research was conducted through a mail survey of 350 firms (250 located in the United States and 100 in Canada) and interviews. Responses to the mail questionnaire were received from 143 firms—a response rate of 40.9%. Interviews were conducted in 18 firms (13 located in the United States and five in Canada). The research also included the development of four case studies. These case studies are presented in the respective appendices.

This is the seventh release from a continuing research effort in the area of business decision processes. Its main purpose is to explore the potential for developing a management accounting system consistent with the actual decision processes and managerial uses of accounting information. This research effort is co-sponsored by the National Association of Accountants and The Society of Management Accountants of Canada.

Our current studies within this research effort deal with the decision processes designated in the initial research phase which resulted in three releases published in 1975-76. The current empirical (descriptive) phase has so far resulted in four published reports, including this one. Another report, *The Pricing Decision,* will be issued in the near future.

iii

343874

Guidance in the preparation of this report was kindly and generously supplied by the Project Committee:

Dwight H. Davis, Chairman
A. O. Smith Corp.
Kankakee, Ill.

John L. Hanson
Electro Corp.
Sarasota, Fla.

Carl M. Koontz
ALCOA
Alcoa, Tenn.

William E. Langdon
The Society of Management Accountants of Canada
Hamilton, Ontario

Thomas P. Montgomery
Ernst & Whinney
Syracuse, N.Y.

The report reflects the views of the researcher and not necessarily those of the Association or the Society or the Project Committee.

Stephen Landekich
Research Director
National Association of Accountants

Table of Contents

List of Figures

Chapter 1

Introduction

The decision of whether to manufacture a product in-house or purchase it on the outside can have a significant impact on the long-term as well as the day-to-day operations of a firm. It can be an important means to maintain the stability of a firm's work force and an effective weapon to help control unwarranted price increases of purchased goods. This study was designed to examine how firms actually perform a make-or-buy analysis. It also contains recommendations of how a firm might improve the process. The introductory chapter will discuss the background of the project, the research design, summary of findings and the organization of the report.

Background of Project

This project is part of the overall Business Decision Models Project. The following section will describe the Business Decision Models Project and the normative make-buy model developed in an earlier publication of the project.

Business Decision Models

The Business Decision Models Project is an ongoing research effort co-sponsored by the National Association of Accountants and the Society of Management Accountants of Canada. The purpose of the project is to identify managerial information needs through a systematic examination of the decision-making process.

An earlier release in this ongoing research effort was *Normative Models in Managerial Decision-Making.*[1] That monograph contains the essential

---

[1] Lawrence A. Gordon, et al., *Normative Models in Managerial Decision-Making,* National Association of Accountants, New York, and The Society of Management Accountants of Canada, Ontario, Canada, 1975.

ingredients of the decision process, as described in the literature, for nine frequently encountered higher-level nonroutine decisions. Each decision is presented by means of a flowchart and a description of each step in the flowchart. The decisions are: new product, distribution channels, acquisition, divestment (product abandonment), capital expenditure, lease-buy, make-buy, pricing, and manpower planning.

A pilot study[2] and expanded study[3] of *actual* practice in the evaluation of the lease-purchase decision have been published. An empirical study[4] of the distribution channels decision also has been published. The present study is designed to examine actual practice in the evaluation of the make-or-buy alternative.

Make-Buy Normative Model

The make-buy section of *Normative Models in Managerial Decision-Making* comments that there are several methods indicated in the literature for evaluating the make-or-buy alternative. Two of them that seem to be most popular are explained as follows:

> The first is to compare the estimated incremental operating costs of make or buy, where these costs are considered to remain constant over time. This approach usually does not consider the time value of money nor does it consider the implicit costs associated with the decision—e.g., opportunity costs related to the revenues foregone by utilizing existing plant facilities, costs associated with the need for larger inventories, and costs associated with the need for additional working capital.

> The second technique, on the other hand, takes into account all incremental costs—e.g., operating costs, capital expenditures and implicit costs—on a discounted cash flow basis. Since this latter method generally is viewed as the theoretically correct approach, our model is of this type.[5]

The make-buy model, as well as the explanation of the various steps in the flowchart contained in that publication, are reproduced in Appendix B.

---

[2] William L. Ferrara, *The Lease-Purchase Decision: How Some Companies Make It*, National Association of Accountants, New York, and The Society of Management Accountants of Canada, Ontario, Canada, 1978.

[3] William L. Ferrara, et al., *The Lease-Purchase Decision*, National Association of Accountants, New York, and The Society of Management Accountants of Canada, Ontario, Canada, 1980.

[4] Douglas M. Lambert, *The Distribution Channels Decision*, National Association of Accountants, New York, and The Society of Management Accountants of Canada, Ontario, Canada, 1978.

[5] Lawrence A. Gordon, *op. cit.*, p. 75.

Research Design

Research for this study was conducted in four phases:

- Review of the Literature
- Mail Survey
- Interviews
- Case Study Development

The following will discuss how these phases were designed and will present some of the major sources encountered in the literature search.

Review of the Literature

The objectives of the literature survey were to: (1) examine previous works in the area, (2) provide background information for the construction of a mail survey, and (3) identify potential candidates to participate in the study.

The literature search phase of the project was exhaustive. It consisted of a review of substantially all the literature on the subject published primarily in the United States and Canada, going back to the 1950's. The bibliography in this report includes all sources reviewed.

As can be seen from the bibliography, most of the literature is in article form and a good part of it appears in the NAA publication *Management Accounting* and its predecessor *NAA Bulletin.* In 1973, NAA's Management Accounting Practices (MAP) Committee, one of whose purposes is to recommend practices to be followed by management accountants, issued its Statement No. 5, *Criteria for Make-or-Buy Decisions.* Although rather theoretical in nature, it provides detailed guidelines of how this decision should be made.

Because the make-buy decision requires input from many individuals in the firm, particularly from purchasing and engineering, the publications that serve these disciplines were also helpful. The *Journal of Purchasing, Purchasing Magazine,* and a few engineering publications all contained several articles on the subject.

Other major contributors to the field were the American Management Association (AMA) and the National Association of Purchasing Management (NAPM). The AMA has published several books which discuss this subject. The NAPM publishes the magazine *Journal of Purchasing* and has developed an audio-visual presentation. This presentation, developed in 1972, is titled *Make or Buy.* The Leader's Guide to this presentation explores the subject in-depth. It contains a handy formula—the Make-Buy Ratio—that can be used when making this decision. This ratio is discussed in Chapter 3.

Mail Survey

The primary goal of the second phase of the study, the mail survey, was to examine practices followed in the make-or-buy decision. A secondary goal was to identify candidates for the interview phase and the subsequent development of case studies. The questionnaire, contained in Appendix A, was designed to give an overview of the firm's decision process and indicate how sophisticated it was.

To encourage a good response, the questionnaire was brief and the amount of time required to complete it was held to a minimum. It contained only five questions, all of which could be answered by use of check marks.

The first question surveyed whether the firm had a formal or written make-or-buy policy. One of the aims of this question was to help identify participants for subsequent phases of the study.

The literature strongly indicates that this decision requires the participation of many disciplines within the firm. To test how true this was in practice, the second question surveyed which areas usually provide input. The third question asked which function has primary responsibility to make this decision.

One of the reasons the make-or-buy determination is difficult is that there are so many variables which affect it, many of which are nonquantifiable. The fourth question required the participant to identify and rank the relative importance of financial and nonfinancial variables.

The last question was designed to indicate whether full or only marginal (out-of-pocket) costs were more frequently used in the financial evaluation of this decision. A second part assessed whether the time value of money was considered.

The questionnaire was mailed to a total of 350 industrial firms. Of these, 250 were located in the United States, and 100 were in Canada. The U.S. sample was selected from the "Fortune 500." The Canadian firms were taken from a similar Canadian listing, "The Financial Post 300." This listing includes the top 200 Canadian industrial firms, from which selection was made, as well as 100 "other" (mining, financial, etc.), firms. Because the literature and a preliminary analysis of survey responses indicated that the essentials of the decision process did not vary between U.S. and Canadian firms, it was decided that the results would be more meaningful if the responses received from both countries were combined.

The sample was restricted to larger firms because it was expected that they would be more willing to participate, and would more likely be involved with make-or-buy decisions, thus making a greater contribution than smaller firms. Furthermore, the results obtained probably would be applicable to firms of all sizes.

To obtain some variation in size, instead of selecting the largest firms on these lists, *every other firm* in the sales ranking was included in the sample.

4

Thus, the first, third, fifth, etc., largest firms were chosen.

Inasmuch as the participants in the decision most probably varied from firm to firm, the determination of the person to whom the questionnaire should be directed caused a problem. It was decided that it should be directed to the chief financial officer of the firm because as an accountant he probably would be more cooperative than someone in another discipline. The recipient was instructed, in the cover letter, to have it completed by an individual who was best qualified. To facilitate any future contacts, the person completing it was asked at the end of the questionnaire to indicate his name and title.

A second request was mailed to all participants who had not replied to the first. A total of 143 responses were received, which resulted in a favorable response rate of 40.9%. Of these, 19 respondents indicated that this survey was not applicable to them, as they were seldom, if ever, involved in a make-or-buy decision. Thus 124 responses were utilized in the analysis which is contained in Chapter 5.

Interviews

The first question on the mail survey asked whether the firm had a formal or written make-or-buy policy. As indicated in the previous section, one of the purposes of this question was to help identify participants for subsequent phases of the study. To facilitate any future contacts, space was provided at the end of the questionnaire for the individual completing it to indicate his or her name.

It was felt that firms that had formal policies would probably also have more advanced decision processes and thus might make a better contribution to subsequent phases of the study. A total of 39 firms, all of whom were contacted, answered this question affirmatively. Unfortunately, many firms which indicated that they had a formal policy were actually referring to their capital expenditures policy. Ultimately, unstructured interviews were conducted with 18 firms—13 U.S. and five Canadian. As with the mail survey, the interviews indicated that the decision process did not vary between U.S. and Canadian firms.

The interviews initially were conducted with the individual who had completed the questionnaire, and in many cases others involved in the decision process were spoken with. The purpose of the interviews was to examine the decision process at the firm more carefully and identify case studies that could be incorporated in this report. The interview findings are contained throughout the report and in the case studies in the appendices.

Case Study Development

The appendices to this report contain four case studies which illustrate how the decision process is performed at four firms participating in the study.

To maintain confidentiality, such factors as company and product names, quantities, ingredients, and the like have been changed where necessary.

The first case study illustrates how the typical make-or-buy decision is made at Stener Inc. It does this by discussing the workings of Stener's permanent Make/Buy Committee. Included in this discussion are two rather simple flowcharts which indicate the typical steps of a make and a buy study.

The second case contains the make-or-buy plan of Abco Corp., which was part of a bid proposal for a government contract. This case includes a series of make-or-buy studies for various items in a space project. Because the project is highly complex and requires critical interfacing, nonfinancial considerations are most important.

The third case discusses the use of make-buy as part of a continuous program of value analysis. This case assesses whether it would be cheaper to manufacture an item in-house rather than on the outside. This assessment includes only current out-of-pocket costs and uses a discounted cash-flow technique.

The last case is concerned with a make-or-buy study at PM Corp. Due to continuous price increases of one of the parts it purchases, an assessment is made whether it would be advantageous to produce this item in-house. This case represents an extremely thorough make-or-buy study which considers the time value of money and illustrates how this analysis was used to negotiate a reduction in a proposed price increase.

Summary of Findings

This section will briefly discuss the major findings of the study.

The study disclosed that although the make-or-buy determination can have an important effect on the well-being of a firm, it is very often not given sufficient study—probably for two reasons. First, this decision can be rather difficult to properly evaluate because there are a host of factors that must be considered. Many of these factors are highly subjective and difficult to assess and require input from several disciplines. Second, on an individual basis, the dollar amounts involved in typical make-or-buy studies are often small. Thus, they are frequently made informally and by lower-level employees.

The make-or-buy decision is usually made with few guidelines. Although a relatively large (31.5%) portion of the respondents to this study indicated that they have a formal make-buy policy, upon further investigation it was determined that most were referring to make or buy if the decision to make involved the acquisition of equipment. If no capital expenditure were required, the make-or-buy determination would usually be made informally.

The department indicated as *participating* most often in this decision was manufacturing. Rather surprisingly, the second most frequently mentioned

6

department was accounting, which was followed by purchasing, engineering, top management, marketing, and labor relations.

Top management was disclosed to have the *primary responsibility* for making this determination most often. An interdisciplinary committee was a distant second, followed by manufacturing, accounting, purchasing, and engineering. A significant portion (28.2%) indicated that primary responsibility was shared by two or more areas.

There are a variety of factors which should be considered in the make-or-buy decision. Those factors which were considered very or extremely important by participants in descending order were: cost, ROI, investment, dependability of supply, manufacturing capacity, manufacturing expertise, and quality control.

It is evident that there is a great deal of disagreement over whether full or variable costs should be used in the make-buy analysis. This study indicated that the type of costs used varies with the time frame of the decision. Variable costs are generally used for the short term, while full costs are determined for long-term decisions.

Most participants made the make-buy financial determination rather simply. Generally, only current costs were used and inflation or the time value of money often ignored. Examples of more sophisticated analyses which consider the time value of money are included in the appendices.

Organization of Report

This report is organized into six chapters and six appendices. The second chapter contains an overview of the decision process. It discusses such items as the importance and complexity of the decision, influencing factors, participants, and the advantages of making and buying.

Chapter 3 discusses the financial considerations (cost, investment and ROI) that are important to this decision, while a discussion of nonfinancial considerations (level of activity, quality, quantity and the like) are contained in Chapter 4. The questionnaire responses are analyzed in the fifth chapter. Chapter 6 contains the summary and recommendations based on this study.

A copy of the questionnaire and cover letter comprise Appendix A. The make-buy normative model that appeared in *Normative Models in Managerial Decision-Making* is in Appendix B. Appendix C illustrates the working of the permanent make-buy committee at Stener Inc.

The make-or-buy plan developed by Abco Corp., and included in its bid proposal, is illustrated in Appendix D. Appendix E contains Melten's study of whether it should continue to subcontract the manufacturing of Product Q or bring it in-house. Finally, Appendix F contains an in-depth make-or-buy study performed by PM Corp. initiated as a result of continuous price increases of one of its parts.

Chapter 2

Overview of Decision

This chapter contains an overview of the make-or-buy decision. It discusses various aspects of this decision and is designed to make the reader better understand this process. Some of the factors discussed are the decision's importance, complexity, influencing factors, and usual participants. Reproduced at the end of the chapter is the Make-or-Buy Policy of one of the participants.

Importance

The importance of the make-or-buy decision is evidenced by the fact that all manufacturing firms at some time during the course of their operations will probably have to make such a decision. The choice of whether to manufacture an item internally or purchase it on the outside can be applied to a wide variety of decisions—for parts needed for the production of goods for sale, a new building, new equipment, tooling, and the like. Thus, they are often major determinants of profitability and can be significant to the financial health of a company.

Individually, these decisions may or may not produce a significant impact on a firm's operation. However, in the aggregate, they can have a long-range effect on a firm's operating performance. These decisions can affect a firm's production methods and capacities, working capital, cost of borrowing funds, and competitive position.

The objective of a make-or-buy decision should be to best utilize the productive and financial resources of the firm. Despite its importance, "...studies indicate that surprisingly few firms (large or small) give adequate objective study to their make-or-buy problems."[1] This conclusion, made in

---

[1] Lamar Lee, Jr. and Donald W. Dobler, *Purchasing and Materials Management: Text and Cases* (Chapter 15: Make or Buy), McGraw-Hill Book Co., New York, 1977, p. 301.

9

the book *Purchasing and Materials Management,* was definitely confirmed by this research study.

Complexity of Decision

Not only is the make-or-buy decision important to the firm, but it is also a very sensitive and complex process. One of the reasons it is so complicated is that there are a host of factors which must be taken into consideration when making this decision. These factors include financial (quantitative) and nonfinancial (qualitative) considerations.

Financial considerations include the cost and investment involved. Non-financial considerations include quality requirements, vendor relations, work-force stability, and a variety of others which will be discussed throughout the report. In addition to the fact that many considerations must be subjectively assessed, they are constantly changing. Thus this decision is highly volatile.

Although this research project uncovered some cases in which the make-buy decision is made in a rather sophisticated manner, in the majority of cases it was done so in a simplistic manner. The study substantiated the following comment made by Lee and Dobler:

> It is not difficult to find otherwise well-managed firms in which most make-or-buy decisions are inadvertently delegated to a clerk in inventory control or production control. It should now be apparent that this is a poor practice. In the first place, such a person does not normally have adequate information with which to make an intelligent decision from a companywide point of view. Second, even if adequate information were available, a typical clerical employee lacks the breadth of experience to evaluate fully the significance of the information and the resultant decision."[2]

To be made effectively, this decision must be given more serious consideration. The initial phase of a make-or-buy evaluation should be concerned with the establishment and/or recognition of existing goals, capabilities, and limitations which are pertinent to these alternatives. Thus, before the make-buy decision is made, a manufacturing firm should establish a goal based on the nature and extent of its production facilities. At the same time, a firm should also define the manufacturing processes that are in accord with overall company goals and strategies. Establishing these considerations, a firm can proceed to an analysis of the financial and nonfinancial factors of the individual make-buy decisions.

---

[2] *Ibid.*

Volatility of Decision

In properly determining the make-or-buy decision, the possible effect of *all* factors on a firm's operations should be considered. Those factors include diverse cost and noncost considerations. Business activity is usually uncertain and ever-changing. Due to changes in technology, demand, competition and the like, a good decision may become a bad one in a very short time.

As indicated, this decision should be made in concert with a firm's overall goals. As these goals change, so would the influence of certain factors. If a firm considers it essential to stabilize production so that no employee will be laid off during periods of slack production, the make alternative might be favored during these periods. If this policy were changed, the buy decision might be selected. It should be noted, particularly during the interview phase of the study, that it was indicated that work-force stability is an important consideration in the make-buy decision.

Similarly, an "easy money" policy or liberal depreciation and taxing policies would also tend to encourage make decisions. As economic conditions change so would these governmental policies. Thus it should be apparent that make-or-buy evaluations will vary between firms and should be continually updated. This point is summarized well in the following statement by Lee and Dobler:

> Beware of rigid formulas and rules of thumb that claim to produce easy make-or-buy decisions. The make-or-buy question is influenced by a multitude of diverse factors that are in a constant state of change. Under such conditions, few easy decisions turn out well in both the short and the long run. Moreover, the relevant factors vary immensely from one firm to another. For these reasons, every company should periodically evaluate the effectiveness of its past decisions to generate information helpful in guiding future courses of make-buy action.[3]

How Make-Buy Decisions Develop

When faced with a choice between self-manufacturing and purchasing from an outside supplier, the firm has the following alternatives:

- Make an item currently purchased.
- Buy an item currently made.
- Make or buy an item currently not a part of the company's product line.
- Make or buy more or less of an item the company is currently making and/or buying.

---

[3] *Ibid.*

An initial make-or-buy study can originate in a number of ways. Some of these are discussed in the following paragraphs.

The make-or-buy question should be investigated when a new product is being developed or an old one is being substantially modified. While a new product is being planned, this question should be analyzed so as to make optimum use of the firm's resources.

In the case where an item is currently being purchased, unsatisfactory vendor performance might give rise to a make-buy study. Poor performance may be due to failure to provide a product of sufficient quality in the proper quantities. Often unreasonable price increases will trigger such a study. This was the impetus of the make-buy study presented in Case F of the appendix.

Firms often conduct value analyses of existing products. Such an analysis might conclude that it would be better to produce an item in-house rather than to continue to purchase it, for example. This was the cause of the study presented in Case E of the appendix.

Another important factor that could give rise to a make-or-buy decision would be changes in sales volume. Reductions in sales would result in cutbacks in production, idling facilities and manpower. To utilize these facilities and manpower, the firm might attempt to bring previously purchased work in-house. On the other hand, during periods of rising sales and production, make-buy investigations might be conducted to try to increase dependence on outside suppliers.

Factors Influencing the Decision

As indicated, there are host of factors, both financial and nonfinancial, which must be considered when making this decision. These factors include:

Financial
   Cost
   Investment
   ROI

Nonfinancial
   Manufacturing Capacity
   Employment Stability
   Confidentiality of Process
   Quality Control
   Manufacturing Expertise
   Dependability of Supply
   Procurement Lead Time
   Multiple Sources
   Technological Obsolescence

Financial considerations generally are first calculated as a starting point for the make-or-buy determination. The nonfinancial factors are then considered and often are more important than the financial ones. In actuality, there may be a number of additional nonfinancial considerations that have an impact on the decision.

The above list of financial and nonfinancial considerations was included in the questionnaire in the mail survey. The respondent was asked to rate the relative importance of each factor in the firm's make-or-buy study. The following factors were rated as *very important* by most respondents: cost, investment, ROI, manufacturing capacity, quality control, manufacturing expertise, and dependability of supply.

Likewise, most respondents indicated the following factors were *moderately important:* employment stability, procurement lead time, multiple sources, and technological obsolescence. Finally, confidentiality of process was rated to be of little importance by most participants.

Advantages of Making or Buying

This study's mail survey did not assess what participants felt were the primary advantages of buying or of making. A number of past studies did, however, and it is interesting to examine their results. In 1972, the *Purchasing Magazine*[4] conducted such a survey in which a group of its readers were asked this question. According to this study, the most important advantage of buying rather than manufacturing in-house was lower cost. The other reasons for purchasing in descending order of importance were: greater manufacturing expertise, faster delivery, better quality, and greater overall discounts.

The results of the question asking the main advantage of making a part rather than buying it were naturally somewhat different. The responses in descending order of importance were: lower costs, greater control over quality, use of idle machinery, faster delivery, use of excess labor, and retention of secret knowledge.

The March-April 1955 issue of the *Harvard Business Review*[5] contained the results of a similar survey. One of the questions asked the respondent to indicate the major factors influencing the decision to make and to buy. The replies in order of frequency are listed on page 14.

---

[4] Peter Wulff, "Make-or-Buy Decisions Shift Like Quicksand," *Purchasing Magazine,* September 19, 1972, pp. 83-85.

[5] Carter C. Higgins, "Make-or-Buy Re-Examined," *Harvard Business Review,* March-April 1955, pp. 109-115.

Reasons for Buying

- Benefit of outside supplier's specialized abilities
- Less expensive
- Volume not big enough to justify capital and inventory investment
- Plant space
- Demand varies; we buy overflows
- Quicker delivery

Reasons for Making

- Integration of plant operations
- Help carry overhead
- Less expensive
- Unusual complex parts requiring direct supervision
- Higher quality
- Less transportation and delivery delays
- Secrecy (did not want designs widely known)
- Unreliability of suppliers

As can be seen, the reasons for making or buying are diverse and would undoubtedly vary in importance with each decision.

Participants

Because all firms have different organizational structures, participants in a make-or-buy decision would vary between firms. Those business functions that often participate in the decision are marketing, manufacturing, engineering, purchasing, and accounting.

The role of the management accountant should be of major importance in the decision-making process. The management accountant is capable of providing the cost and investment data and evaluating the financial considerations of the decision. As a basis for his or her financial evaluations, the management accountant should rely on the information provided by marketing, manufacturing, engineering, and purchasing. Figure 1 illustrates the decision-making process and the various functional groups.

The decision-making body referred to in Figure 1 has the primary responsibility to make this decision and might be top management, a particular department, or an interdisciplinary committee. One of the questions in the mail survey asked which discipline or department within the firm had the primary responsibility to make this decision. Those disciplines that were selected, in order of frequency, were: top management, interdisciplinary committee, manufacturing, accounting, purchasing, and engineering. The results from this question are described in detail in Chapter 5.

Figure 1

PARTICIPANTS IN MAKE-BUY

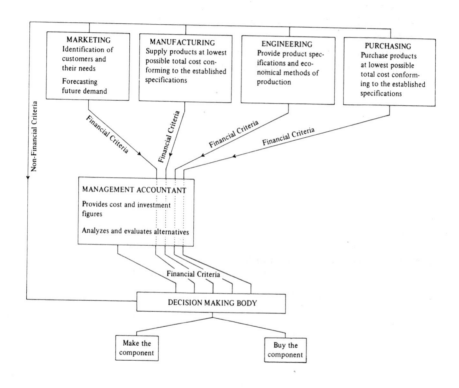

(From Ian D. Duncan, "Make-or-Buy Decisions," *Cost and Management*, September-October 1975, p. 45.)

Because input for the decision comes from so many sources and departments, it was often suggested in the interviews that some sort of interdisciplinary committee should probably administer the decision process. It was further recommended that this committee should include managerial-level representatives of those departments that can contribute to the decision or are affected by it.

Formal Policy

Another question on the mail survey asked whether the firm had a formal make-or-buy policy. Although a surprisingly large number, 31.5%, indicated that they did, it became apparent that this figure was too high. Upon further investigation, it was found that many respondents were actually referring to their capital expenditures policy, which only mentioned make-buy briefly, if at all. Those make-buy policies that were investigated generally treated the subject incompletely.

The make-or-buy policy of one of the participants is reproduced in its entirety on the following pages. Unlike most, it treats the subject very thoroughly and provides an excellent guide for making this decision at the BCO Corporation.

Subject: Make-or-Buy Policy of BCO Corporation

1.   *Purpose*

1.1   To provide guidance to Manufacturing & Engineering Group Headquarters and Divisional Management in arriving at a correct make-or-buy decision.

2.   *Scope*

2.1   The policies set forth herein will apply to all units of the Manufacturing & Engineering (M & E) Group.

3.   *Definition*

3.1   The term make-or-buy is meant to include either of the following types of decision situations:

A M & E Group decision is made between the alternatives of manufacturing within one or more of the M & E Group facilities or of purchasing from other sources.

A divisional decision is made between the alternatives of manufacturing product items within a division for its own use or application or of purchasing from another source.

4.   *Responsibility*

4.1   Make-or-Buy decisions will be the responsibility of management as designated herein:

4.1.1   The decision will be made by Vice President, M & E Group, when any of the following conditions exist:

The product item is to be restricted within divisions of the M & E Group. (See Manufacturing & Engineering Group Manual Subject 5.1 for restricted items policy.)

Approval of a capital investment is required for a "make" decision and as such shall be subject to the Capital Appropriation Request policy as stated in Corporate Controllers Manual Subject 5.2.2.

The decision involves issues other than cost of a product. (Note paragraphs 7 and 8.)

4.2   The decision to make-or-buy will be made by Division General Manager when all of the following conditions are met:

The item in question will be used only within the division making the decision.

The whole cost to manufacture does not exceed the total cost to purchase.

No capital investment is required to carry out the decision.

The item to be made is within the present general scope of the division requiring no major expansion of new skills, techniques or equipment.

5.   *Evaluation Procedure*

5.1   The make-or-buy decision will be made by an evaluation of all pertinent facts to determine that alternative which provides the best long-term advantage for the Corporation.

5.2   When M & E Group Headquarters approval of a divisional recommendation to manufacture an item is required, the division will send a specific recommendation with full details to the Vice President—M & E Group, who will advise the division manager of the decision.

5.3   A divisional recommendation shall include:

All information influencing the decision with a complete breakdown of planned costs in sufficient detail for careful analysis of full costs as well as "out of pocket" costs.

Up-to-date quotations from outside sources sufficient to provide a basis for comparison.

An explanation in detail of the determining factors if other than lowest cost.

Possibility of selling the item outside the Corporation.

6.   *Additional Considerations*

6.1   Various corporate and divisional objectives may influence the make-or-buy decision. The weight given these objectives will vary from time to time depending upon circumstances. Among the factors to be commonly considered are the following:

Reduction of unit cost of finished product

Optimum utilization of available facilities and skills

Reduction of current capital investments to provide for other utilization of available funds

Stabilization of employment levels

Assurance of a basic source of supply

Protection of proprietary information or techniques

Development of or check on "state of the art"

Improvement or control of quality

Development or maintenance of a specific group of skilled labor

6.2   Among other make-or-buy decision factors affecting a specific condition which must also be considered in making a decision are the following:

6.2.1   Labor Relations conditions:
Level and ratio of skilled and non-skilled personnel required. A significant shift in labor.
New skills required. Labor market.

6.2.2   Customer Relations conditions:
The product being presently supplied to us by a customer
Entering the market in competition against a customer

6.2.3   Vendor Relations conditions:
The effect on our ability to buy other materials
The effect on our ability to check competitive prices

6.2.4   Technical Assistance conditions:
The effect of technical assistance, normally supplied by the vendor, being no longer available

Our technical capability to remain competitive with the product under consideration

The risks involved in rapid changes in the state of the art, design and production application

6.2.5   Product Planning conditions:

The effect on long-term objectives for products and product mix. The requirements for engineering and manufacturing capability consistent with long-term requirements. How the product fits into our present marketing capability if its sale is involved.

6.2.6   Other conditions:

The diversion of funds on a make decision restricting their use for other purposes. Management and technical capabilities detrimentally diverted from more critical or productive areas. Raw material availability in sufficient quantities. Patent or other legal problems involved.

7.   *Considerations as to Partial Make or Buy*

7.1   Frequently, for various reasons, it may be advisable both to purchase and manufacture a part and in general, the following alternatives are available:

Make a quantity less than the least anticipated requirement and buy a portion of our requirements thus retaining a contact with the market.

Make a quantity less than the normal amount required and buy a portion of our requirements at all times except when production is on the low side of the cycle.

Make our normal requirements, buying a portion only during periods of unusual demand. However, under such a plan, we could be buying in a seller's market and a satisfactory supply might be difficult to purchase with no regular source.

7.2   It may be desirable, where the need exists and the volume will permit, to purchase a portion of an item which we normally manufacture in order to appraise current market prices. The percentage of the total requirement to be purchased under these circumstances may vary with each item.

7.3   All make-or-buy decisions shall be reviewed periodically to determine the soundness of the basic decision and the extent to which it has stood the test of time.

Chapter 3

Financial Considerations

This study strongly indicates that financial considerations, while important, are often not the primary considerations in the make-buy evaluation. Often nonfinancial factors are more important. A discussion of nonfinancial considerations is contained in Chapter 4. This chapter will discuss the financial considerations of (1) cost, (2) investment, and (3) ROI.

Cost

Although cost is often not the most important consideration in determining make or buy, it usually offers a good starting point in making this determination. In addition, it is probably the area where the accountant provides the greatest input.

Problems in Proper Determination

There are many problems involved in the determination of costs for make or buy. First, the cost to manufacture an item that is currently being bought can only be estimated. This estimate will vary depending upon the type of cost that is available, the treatment of overhead, the activity level of the plant, and other such factors. If new facilities are to be purchased, there are the added questions of how depreciation is to be handled and what allowance should be made for the training of production personnel. Thus, many questions must be settled before definite figures can be calculated.

An added problem is that to insure accurate analysis, all of the factors (quality, specifications, quantity, and the like) must be identical for both alternatives. Even if these factors were identical for an item purchased or manufactured in-house, which is highly unlikely, the cost to manufacture would be only an estimate. Thus, the comment was made that if all factors are equal, and there is only a slight advantage in favor of making, the item would probably be purchased. This situation is so because more reliance would be put on a *known* cost rather than an *estimated* one.

Use of Direct vs. Full Costs

This study indicates that there is a great deal of disagreement over which costs should be included in the analysis. Many persons hold that only direct or variable costs are relevant to the decision, while others maintain full (fixed + variable) costs should be considered.

Variable Costs

Variable costs are those costs that vary in direct proportion to the quantity purchased or manufactured. Variable costs can be broken down between *direct variable costs* and *direct variable overhead. Direct variable costs* are those items that should be part of manufacturing costs. They would include direct material, direct labor and related costs, and subcontract work in case of unusually tight production capacity.[1]

The components of overhead that would be included in *direct variable overhead* are more numerous and difficult to define. Those items in this category that would be relevant to a make-buy study would include the following manufacturing expenses: material handling, indirect labor, fringe benefits, overtime premium, supervision, power, special training costs, set-up and tear-down time for conversion of equipment, and equipment depreciation.

The following is a summary of the major variable cost items that should be included in an estimate to make or to buy:

To Make

Delivered raw material costs
Direct labor costs (including inspection costs)
Incremental factory overhead costs
Incremental managerial costs
Incremental purchasing costs
Incremental inventory carrying costs
Incremental costs of capital

To Buy

Purchase price of the part
Transportation costs
Receiving and inspection costs[2]

---

[1] Myron J. Hubler, Jr., "The Make or Buy Decision," *Management Services,* November-December 1966, p. 47.

[2] Lamar Lee, Jr., and Donald W. Dobler, *Purchasing and Materials Management: Text and Cases,* (Chapter 15: Make or Buy), McGraw-Hill Book Company, New York, 1977, p. 304.

Fixed Costs

Fixed costs are those costs that are not influenced by the volume of items purchased or manufactured. NAA's Management Accounting Practices (MAP) Committee in *Criteria for Make-or-Buy Decisions* defines fixed costs as:

> ...the aggregate of all cost elements directly and indirectly assignable to support a specific cost objective on a long-term going concern basis under which every aspect of business activity bears its proper portion of all costs and all costs are assigned to specific cost objectives.[3]

Fixed costs might include some items mentioned above in *direct variable overhead* which in fact do not vary at a particular firm. In addition they might include such items as building repairs and maintenance, insurance, general taxes, and administrative costs.

The Effect of Capacity

The determination of the most appropriate cost concept (full or variable) to use in a make-or-buy analysis would appear to depend on the level of operation and capacity at a firm. The effect of the level of activity on cost will be discussed in the next chapter. This section will discuss the behavior of full or variable costs at different levels of capacity.

Let us assume that a firm that has been purchasing widgets now wishes to manufacture them. Upon investigation, it is revealed that the firm is working at 100% capacity and will continue to do so for the foreseeable future. If the firm does bring the widgets in-house, additional facilities would have to be obtained. In this case, there would be an increase in variable costs plus fixed overhead caused by the in-house production of widgets.

On the other hand, let us assume that this firm has excess capacity for the foreseeable future. Thus, production can be brought in-house with the existing facilities. In this case, there would be only an increase in the variable costs due to widget production. Fixed costs are sunk and will continue regardless of whether production is brought in-house. In fact, in the case of idle capacity, the utilization of excess capacity results in a decrease in *unit* cost. This is due to the additional production absorbing some of the fixed overhead. This can be illustrated in the graph in Figure 2 which was included in the Make or Buy chapter of *Purchasing and Materials Management*.

The graph indicates that a 12½% increase in production (from 80% to 90% of capacity) is achieved by a total cost increase of only 10%. This

---

[3] National Association of Accountants, *Statements on Management Accounting Practices: Criteria for Make-or-Buy Decisions,* Statement No. 5, Author, New York, June 22, 1973, p. 2.

situation resulted because only variable costs increased while unused capacity was utilized.

Let us now assume that sufficient excess capacity existed for the production of widgets only for the first and second years. In the third year and thereafter, all excess capacity would be used and new facilities required. In a determination of additional costs to manufacture, the authors recommend that fixed costs not be included in the analysis for the first two years. Subsequently, the cost of widget production should include the increase in fixed costs that it will cause.

To summarize, if the plant has excess capacity, increases in production will result mainly in an increase in variable costs. If a plant is fully utilized, an increase in production can be accomplished only by increasing capacity, thereby adding both fixed and variable costs.

Figure 2

INCREMENTAL COSTS

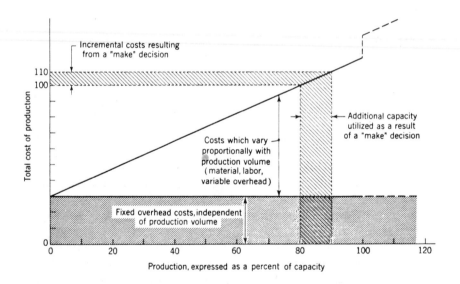

(From Lamar Lee, Jr. and Donald W. Dobler, *Purchasing and Materials Management: Text and Cases,* (Chapter 15: Make or Buy), McGraw-Hill Book Company, New York, 1977, p. 306.)

The Debate

The study indicated there is a continuing debate as to whether the direct or full-cost concept should be used in the analysis of make-buy. Although many writers feel that the concept used should vary with the circumstances, such as the availability of capacity, others seem to feel only one concept should be used exclusively.

NAA's MAP Committee in the Statement, *Criteria for Make-or-Buy Decisions,* discusses the use of variable and full costs in this decision. The Committee takes the position that full costs should be used in *all* make-or-buy analyses.

It is concluded that in the case of short-term decisions, variable costs become more significant. However:

> ...it is recommended that the long-term and full-cost considerations also be developed. The short-term judgments can then be properly evaluated against the alternative choices which will be required at a later date.[4]

The application of the full-cost concept in *all* cases would reduce uncertainties caused by evaluating the time frame of the decision involved. In addition to present costs, the MAP Committee recommends that a make-or-buy analysis should give consideration to what *future* costs are expected to be.

The following checklist from the MAP Statement contains the more significant cost elements to be included in the alternative to make or to buy. It is suggested that each element be further classified into that portion that will have an immediate incremental impact and that portion that is fixed in nature and assigned.[5]

Cost to Buy	*Cost to Make*
Administration	Administration
	Direct Manufacturing Costs
Engineering	Engineering
Freight and Duties	Freight and Duties
Inspection	
	Indirect Manufacturing Costs
Insurance and Taxes	
Inventory Carrying Costs—	Inventory Carrying Costs—
(But not the cost of investment in inventory which is included as a part of total investment)	(But not the cost of investment in inventory which is included as a part of total investment)

---

[4]National Association of Accountants, *op. cit.,* p. 6.

[5]*Ibid.,* pp. 8-9.

Cost to Buy	Cost to Make
Invoice Cost	
Invoice Processing	Invoice Processing
	Manufacturing Variances
	Material Handling
Patterns, Dies and Molds	Patterns, Dies and Molds
Purchasing	Purchasing
Quality Assurance	Quality Assurance
Receiving and Handling	
Research and Development	Research and Development
	Start-up Costs
Tooling	Tooling

Regardless of the cost concept used, to insure a proper make-or-buy analysis:

> ...the cost element must be specifically identified with the cost objectives related to the evaluation of clearly defined alternative courses of action. Thus, it is essential that complete and accurate determination be made of the specific costs related to the alternative to *make* and the alternative to *buy*... cost to make vs. cost to buy must be based on the same assumptions. Thus, costs for each of the alternatives must be based on the identical product specifications, quantities and quality standards.[6]

The first part of the fifth question on the mail survey asked whether the firm uses full or marginal (direct) costs in the make-buy evaluation. Approximately 44% of the respondents indicated they used full costs. A little less than 39% indicated marginal, while almost 18% included the category "both" in their response.

Actual Practice

Both the mail survey and the interviews indicated that, in practice, variable costs are generally used for short-term decisions while full costs are used for long-term decisions. Sometimes *both* are calculated regardless of the time frame involved.

Generally, variable cost analysis was considered sufficient in the determination of whether to manufacture a purchased item on a temporary basis, if excess capacity were available. In this case, cost considerations dictated that the item be brought in-house if the variable cost to manufacture is less than the purchase cost. This is so because the production of the item would not result in an increase in fixed overhead.

It was mentioned in several instances that in the case of idle capacity, a purchased item might be brought in-house temporarily even though its variable costs to manufacture are *greater* than its purchase price. This case

---

[6]*Ibid.*, p. 5.

was often true at a firm involved in seasonal production that wishes to smooth production and not lay off employees. In making a decision for the long term, particularly if the operational policy of the firm will be affected, full costs were generally used in the make-buy analysis.

Several participants indicated that *future,* not current costs, are relevant to the decision and should be used in the analysis. In an attempt to estimate these future costs, such factors as inflation, technological changes, and the like are considered. This process is usually done in a rather subjective manner.

Illustration

This section will illustrate how make-buy data are accumulated on two forms contained in Figures 3 and 4. Although they are taken from the literature, they are presented here because they represent an excellent example of how the same decision should be assessed for both the short term (Figure 3) as well as long term (Figure 4).

The short-term analysis considers only the increase in direct materials, direct labor and variable overhead that would result if the item were manufactured. As can be seen, variable costs would increase $12.69/unit while the purchase price for this quantity would be $40.00/unit. Thus, depending upon other factors, particularly capacity considerations, it would seem to be advantageous to self-manufacture for the short term.

The long-term analysis includes a detailed comparison of full manufacturing cost and the cost to purchase. According to this analysis, the profit to the vendor is indicated as $7.50, whereas the firm would be able to save $10.46/unit ($25.00 – $14.54) if it manufactures the item. Thus, due to self-manufacturing, the firm would save the vendor's profit plus an additional $2.96/unit. The analysis for the long term would also appear to favor the make alternative.

The Make-Buy Ratio

The National Association of Purchasing Management (NAPM) has prepared an audio-visual presentation which explores the subject of make or buy in-depth.[7] Its purpose is to assist a purchasing manager to better make this decision. Included in the presentation is an interesting formula—the make-buy cost ratio. This ratio was designed to give a quick estimate of the cost of each alternative.

---

[7] National Association of Purchasing Management, *Make or Buy,* No. 38, Leaders Guide, Author, New York, 1972.

Figure 3

MAKE-OR-BUY ANALYSIS
SHORT TERM

Department# _472_
Project or Part # XP_250469_
Usage Forecast _100_
Est. Std. Cost/Unit _12.69_
Date Needed _12-1-79_
Lot Quantity _10_

☐ Make   ☒ Buy
Date _10-15-79_
Prepared By _S. Ray_
Approved By _R. Fith_
Estimated Savings _N/A_
Total DLSH _N/A_

	Reliance Manufactured Unit Cost
MAKE	
A. DIRECT VARIABLE COSTS: Note A	
1. Material - Include Variations	$ 9.70
2. Labor - Include Variations as Needed	1.43
a) Set-up	
b) Fringe Costs	
_____ DLSH @ Rate _____	
3. Subcontract	
B. OVERHEAD (INCLUDE SPECIFIC INCREMENTAL COSTS AS NEEDED)	
1. Material Handling	$
2. Indirect Labor	
3. Hourly Supervision	
4. Training (Include special skills)	
5. Overtime Premium	
6. Tooling	
7. Supplies	
8. Other Variable Costs:	
_____	1.56
Total Reliance Costs	$ 12.69

BUY

A. VENDOR INVOICE OR QUOTATION

	Vendor	Delivery Time	Unit Cost
1.	XYZ Co.	3 weeks from order	40.00
2.			
3.			

OTHER

A. CHECK STATUS FROM ONE OF THE FOLLOWING:
1. ☐ New Part
2. ☐ New Part which Replaces an Existing Part
3. ☒ Purchased Part
4. ☐ Reliance Manufactured Part

B. WORKSHEET ATTACHED:
☒ Exhibit I
☒ Exhibit II

C. SPECIAL OR EXTRAORDINARY TOOLING
CHARGES SHOULD BE INCLUDED
☒ YES   ☐ NO

COMMENTS
Welding fixtures required will be unavailable
for 6-8 weeks. Part should be re-evaluated if
there is a larger usage forecast.

NOTE A: Separate departmental labor hour overhead rates may be preferable to the use of composite rates.

(From Myron J. Hubler, Jr., "Make or Buy Decisions," in *Financial Executives Handbook* (R. F. Vancil, ed.) Dow Jones-Irwin, Homewood, Ill., 1970, p. 299.)

Figure 4

MAKE-OR-BUY ANALYSIS
LONG TERM

Department# _472_
Project or Part #_XP250469_
Usage Forecast _10,000_
Est. Std. Cost/Unit _14.54_
Date Needed _12-1-79_
Lot Quantity _1000_

☒ Make ☐ Buy
Date _10-15-79_
Prepared By _C. Ray Sutherland_
Approved By _C. Burns_
Estimated Savings _10.46/unit_
Total DLSH _5.200_

Worksheet Attached
Exhibit I ☒
Exhibit II ☒

	Outside Purchased Unit Cost	Reliance Manufactured Unit Cost
A. DIRECT VARIABLE COSTS - NOTE A:		
1. Material - Include Variations	$ 8.00	$ 9.70
2. Labor - Include Variations		1.45
Reroute		
Shift Premium		
Set-up _3 hours/1,000 units_	1.50	.01
Fringe Costs		
Incentive Pay		
Etc.		
3. Subcontract _- Uncertain at this time_		
B. OVERHEAD (INCLUDE SPECIFIC INCREMENTAL COSTS AS NEEDED)		
1. Material Handling		.10
2. Indirect Labor		
3. Hourly Supervision		.05
4. Training - Include Special Skills		
5. Overtime Premium		
6. Vacation and Holiday Pay		
7. Tooling _$375.00 estimated ÷ 10,000 units_		.04
8. Supplies		
9. Other variable costs:		
Overhead Rate	1.50	2.11
C. SEMI-VARIABLE AND FIXED COSTS - NOTE B:		
Storage Facilities, 1,000 ft.²	1.50	.50
@ $10.00/ft.² - 2 yrs. (Reliance only)		
Freight to Vendor	7.50	
D. OTHER COSTS AND EXPENSES - NOTE C:		
1. _Procurement, Storage, Shipping & Testing_	3.00	.20
2. Division Administration	1.00	.20
3. Division Engineering	3.00	.20
TOTALS	$ 25.00 (Note D)	$ 14.54

COMMENTS

1 extra person will be required - will be split between PST, Admin. & Engrg.

Check Part Status From One of the Following:

1. New Part ☐   2. New Part which replaces an existing part ☐

3. Purchased Part ☒   4. Reliance Manufactured Part ☐

A. Separate departmental labor hour and overhead rates may be preferable to the use of composite rates. The divisional rate for overhead applied should be re-determined as substantial amounts of direct labor hours are absorbed in the make or buy products.

B. Semi-variable and fixed costs such as tooling, depreciation, etc. may be included for specific items.

C. These incremental and out-of-pocket costs are included only when quantities being considered are very high, e.g., 5% of total labor is eliminated by use of the purchased part.

D. Includes vendor's invoice price and adjustments for out-of-pocket non-compensating costs included in the manufactured column.

(From Myron J. Hubler, Jr., "Make or Buy Decisions," in *Financial Executives Handbook* (R. F. Vancil, ed.), Dow Jones-Irwin, Homewood, Ill., 1970, p. 300.)

NAPM suggests that a make-buy cost ratio be developed for each department or operation. This ratio for each alternative can be calculated in two steps.

First, the variable costs of the making department must be established and expressed as a function of its direct labor. This is the burden factor for that department. Second, the variable costs of the purchasing function are calculated in terms of purchased dollars. This determines the purchasing burden factor. The make-buy cost ratio is the ratio between these burden factors.

Let us assume that variable costs of the producing department are $2.75, for each $1.00 of direct labor cost. The burden factor for this department is 3.75 ($2.75 + $1.00 ÷ $1.00). The purchasing burden factor can be determined in a similar fashion. Assuming that variable costs of the purchasing department are $.25 for $1.00 worth of materials purchased, its burden factor would be 1.25 ($.25 + $1.00 ÷ $1.00). Based on these figures, the make-buy ratio would be 3 to 1 (3.75 ÷ 1.25). This problem can be illustrated in the following determination of whether a casting should be machined in-house or bought finished on the outside.

Let us assume that the burden factors for in-house production and purchasing are those calculated above. If the raw casting costs $1.00 per unit, and machining costs $.25 each, total in-house cost can be estimated as the sum of (1) and (2) below:

(1) Raw materials price	×	purchasing burden factor	
$1.00	×	1.25	= $1.25
(2) Machining costs	×	manufacturing burden factor	
$.25	×	3.75	= $ .94
			$2.19

Thus, the unit cost of in-house manufacturing is estimated to be $2.19.

Assuming that the cost of a finished machine casting is $1.50 per unit, the total cost of the purchase option can be determined by multiplying this amount by the purchasing department's burden factor of 1.25.

Purchase cost	×	purchasing burden factor	
$1.50	×	1.25	= $1.88

In this case purchasing, or "buying the labor on the outside," would save $.31 ($2.19 − $1.88) per unit.

Furthermore, if the cost of the raw material ($1.00) would be the same to the supplier as it would be for in-house manufacturing, it can be ignored in the calculation. Thus one can quickly make this decision by determining and comparing the costs of inside labor and purchased labor as follows:

Inside labor cost × machining costs × manufacturing burden factor, or $.25 × 3.75 = $.94.

Purchased labor cost = purchase price (less cost of raw casting) × purchasing burden factor, or $.50 × 1.25 = $.63.

This results in the same advantage in buying rather than making of $.31 per unit ($.94 − $.63). In fact it would be advantageous to go outside if the purchased labor costs up to $.75 per unit ($.75 − 1.25 = $.94). This confirms the 3:1 make-buy ratio (purchased labor cost of $.75 divided by inside labor cost of $.25).

It should be noted that this provides only a quick fix on costs and should be used only as a rough guide. Before any action is taken, a more detailed analysis of costs and other considerations should be made. In addition, because this ratio does not consider fixed costs, it should not be used if they would change.

Investment

Besides costs, a second important financial consideration in make-buy is the amount of investment required. The following discussion covers the concepts of incremental and full investment and indicates actual practice in the area.

Incremental Investment

In the book *Make or Buy*, Gross presents a table, shown as Figure 5, page 32, which accumulates the investment required to make and to buy.

It should be noted that inasmuch as additional facilities were not required, this table considers only the changes (increments) in elements of working capital of the make and the buy alternative. Obviously, if the make alternative required additional facilities, this amount would have to be included in the analysis.

Full Investment

As with cost analysis, the MAP Committee in its Statement suggests that a firm should follow the "Full Investment" concept. It is stated that:

> Investment considerations should not be limited to facilities or equipment but must include the total of direct and indirect uses of company resources which might otherwise be available for alternative purposes.... this "full investment" concept... requires the assignment of all applicable investment directly and indirectly related to the specific investment objectives.[8]

Figure 5

ANALYSIS OF INVESTMENT

	Amounts For "Make"	Amounts For "Buy"	Projection Basis
Total Volume:			
Number of Units	10,000	10,000	Based on Marketing Forecast
Material Costs	$ 18,500	$207,500	
Investment Required:			
Cash	650	3,400	15% of Accounts Receivable and Accrued Items
Inventories			
Receiving	660	6,920	Average 12 Days Required
In Process	16,830	-0-	Average 60 Days Value
Finished Goods	6,230	7,330	12 Days Total Costs
Tooling Costs	7,500	-0-	Average Cost
Total Required	31,870	17,650	
Less: Funds Sources			
Accounts Payable	1,030	12,970	20 Days Terms for Material
Accrued Payroll	1,480	410	Labor Costs, 1 week
Total Sources	2,510	13,380	
Net Investment	29,360	4,270	

(From Harry Gross, *Make or Buy*, Prentice-Hall, Inc., Englewood Cliffs, N.J., 1966, pp. 139.)

---

[8] National Association of Accountants, *op. cit.,* p. 9.

32

Thus existing capacity, which currently is idle but might be used for alternative purposes, should be included as part of the investment to make. In addition, rather than using current conditions, it is recommended that:

> Full consideration must be given to what the investment "should be" under obtainable conditions and reflecting all possible improvements. Thus, the required investment should reflect the best obtainable productivity and efficiency and the lowest possible inventory levels. Investment related to the 'buy' alternative must reflect maximum use of supplier terms, opportunities for suppliers to carry backup inventories, etc.[9]

The following list contains the more significant investment elements to be included in each alternative.[10]

Investment to Buy	*Investment to Make*
Accounts Payable to Suppliers	Accounts Payable to Suppliers
	Accrued Payrolls
Inventory	Inventory
	Manufacturing Facilities
Molds and Dies	Molds and Dies
Office & Service Facilities	Office & Service Facilities
Supplier Credit Terms	Supplier Credit Terms
Warehousing Facilities	Warehousing Facilities

The study of actual practice indicates that firms generally consider only incremental investment in their make-buy study. Furthermore, investment is usually limited to additional capital expenditures that would be required for the make alternative. Some participants suggest, however, that the changes in working capital for both alternatives should be included as well. These changes would be due to higher or lower inventory levels that would be required, increases or decreases in payables, and the like.

ROI

Once costs and investment have been determined, one can calculate the relative return on investment (ROI) of each project. This section will discuss various methods that might be used and the time frame of the evaluation period.

---

[9] *Ibid.*, p. 10.
[10] *Ibid.*, p. 11.

Methods

There are several techniques that can be used to determine the profitability of an investment. They include: payback, average rate of return, net present value, and internal rate of return.

The first two methods, payback and average rate of return, do not consider the time value of money, whereas net present value and the internal rate of return do and are therefore considered superior.

In the present value technique, the firm's cost of capital is used as a discount rate and applied against the project's net cash flow. If the present value of the cash inflows exceeds the cash outflows, the project's return is greater than the firm's cost of capital and the project should be considered.

The internal rate of return is often called the discounted cash flow rate of return. It is that rate at which the present value of the cash inflows equals the present value of cash outflows.

Time Frame

The determination of the period of time in which a project is to be evaluated is necessary to calculate its ROI. This time frame depends on the economic life of the project. The economic life of a product or asset is the shortest of its (1) physical life, (2) technological life, or (3) product-market life.[11]

Although the technological or product-market life of an item may be difficult to estimate, it should be considered for a sound make-or-buy decision. The MAP Committee states that:

> When the decision being reached is to make a part presently purchased and specialized new facilities and/or machines are needed to manufacture the part, then the technological life of the product becomes extremely important. Reasonable assurance is necessary that the part will not become obsolete in the foreseeable future.[12]

The study indicates that the overwhelming majority of firms utilize either the present value or the internal rate of return methods. Two of the case studies at the end of this report include cash flow analyses which calculate the ROI of the respective project. Each of these analyses discounts the increase in cash flow that would result from a decision to make an item presently being purchased. Melten Inc. uses a ten-year period and calculates the present value and internal rate of return. PM Corp. uses a 15-year period and calculates the payback period as well.

---

[11] *Ibid.*, p. 13.
[12] *Ibid.*

Chapter 4

Nonfinancial Considerations

This study strongly disclosed that nonfinancial considerations are often the primary determinants of make or buy. This chapter discusses the influence of some of the major nonfinancial factors on this evaluation. The first such factor, which is discussed at some length, is level of activity. The factors of quality, quantity and dependability of supply are then covered. The above discussions will treat a host of various other nonfinancial considerations. They include, among others: production smoothing, the effect of capacity, production control, manufacturing expertise and multiple sources.

Level of Activity

The level of activity at a plant has an important impact on the decision to make or buy. The following sections deal with the effect of activity on costs, the problem of smoothing production, and coping with uncertainty in future levels of production.

Effect on Costs

The effect of various levels of production on incremental costs is illustrated in the graph in Figure 6.

Total costs (fixed and variable) are graphed along the vertical axis, while percentage of capacity is on the horizontal. The cost at zero capacity represents the startup cost of a new plant. As production approaches a normal level, due to the absorption of fixed overhead, incremental costs will decrease. As utilization exceeds normal and approaches full capacity, the cost to produce an additional unit begins to increase.

The vertical line at the right-hand side of the graph represents the maximum capacity of existing facilities. The dotted line above and to the right of maximum capacity represents a shift in capacity. This is caused by the renting of additional space, equipment additions, and the like.

Figure 6

EFFECT OF INCREMENTAL COSTS AT ALL LEVELS OF CAPACITY

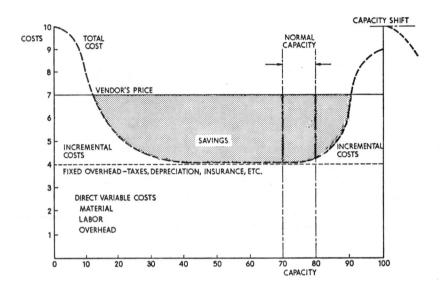

(From Myron J. Hubler, Jr., "Make or Buy Decisions," in *Financial Executives Handbook* (R. F. Vancil, ed.), Dow Jones-Irwin, Homewood, Ill., 1970, p. 302.)

The top unbroken horizontal line represents the vendor's price (the purchase cost). The shaded area between it and the total incremental cost line represents the potential saving to the firm as a result of the decision to manufacture.

It should be noted that the areas from 10% to 40% of capacity and from 70% to 95% of capacity in the above chart have special significance to the make-or-buy decision. This is so because in these areas incremental cost is extremely sensitive to shifts in volume. Thus, at these levels the firm should carefully review and revise its cost estimates and alternatives for making or buying.

Production Smoothing

The desire to maintain production at a fairly constant rate, or production smoothing, can have an important effect on the make-or-buy evaluation. When a firm reaches its full production capacity, it has the alternative to expand or purchase from outsiders any additional requirements. Particularly where future demand is not certain, rather than invest in additional facilities which may not remain fully utilized, the buy option is often favored. In such a case, the firm will produce the items it does so most profitably and temporarily purchase the balance of its requirements from the outside. Likewise during slack periods, rather than facing idle capacity and the need to lay off workers, items which are currently being purchased will be brought in-house.

The mail survey questioned the importance of employment stability in the make-buy decision. Almost 42% of the respondents indicated that it was of moderate importance. At the same time, 36.5% claimed it was of little importance. In subsequent discussions it became clear that the importance of this factor often varied with the skill of the work force. In those firms with a highly skilled work force, employment stability was an extremely important consideration.

During this study it became apparent that because of the uncertainties of future requirements, it is often difficult to develop a production smoothing plan. In the article "Quantitative Analysis and the Make-or-Buy Decision"[1] Shore discusses an interesting model which uses the make-or buy decision to smooth production. The article develops a table which indicates a plan that combines in-house production and outside purchasing to smooth production and minimize total cost.

Dealing with Uncertainty in the Level of Production

Expected future levels of production of an item have an important influence on the results of a make-or-buy analysis. There is, however, often a great deal of uncertainty as to what this future level will be. In the article "Coping With Uncertainty in the Make or Buy Decision,"[2] Doney presents a quantitative technique which attempts to account for this uncertainty. The article presents a hypothetical situation in which a firm is contemplating the manufacture of a part that it uses in one of its finished products. Using subjective probability the author is able to determine the total cost of the make and buy alternatives at different activity levels.

Quality

In many cases, the quality of an item would not differ in any important respect whether it was purchased from an outside vendor or manufactured

---

[1] Barry Shore, "Quantitative Analysis and the Make-or-Buy Decision," *Journal of Purchasing,* February 1970, pp. 5-11.

[2] Lloyd D. Doney, "Coping with Uncertainty in the Make or Buy Decision," *Management Accounting,* October 1968, pp. 31-34.

in-house. In these cases, quality would not be an important factor in the make-or-buy decision. Where there is a significant quality difference between the two alternatives, however, this factor often outweighs all others in this decision.

The mail survey included a question which asked the importance of quality control considerations in the make-or-buy decision. Almost half of the respondents disclosed that it was either very or extremely important.

This study indicated that there are a great many arguments in reference to quality that favor either making or buying. The succeeding pages will first discuss some arguments which favor making, to be followed by those that favor buying.

Favor Making

Two important arguments based on quality which favor making are that the desired quality is not available on the outside and that the firm would have better control of the quality of an item produced in-house.

Cannot Be Purchased

Probably the strongest reason related to quality for making an item is that the desired quality cannot be bought. The following case, Carrigan Manufacturing Company, is taken from Culliton's *Make or Buy*. It is presented here because it is an excellent illustration of the actions taken by a firm that needed a product of specific quality. This firm was unable to locate a supplier that could furnish buffing compounds, for finishing, of satisfactory quality.

> The Carrigan Manufacturing Company . . . manufactured a wide line of metal products. Approximately 10% of the company's sales was composed of products that required the use of buffing compounds for finishing. . . . As a result of the finishing department's dissatisfaction with the quality of compound then being purchased, the company's purchasing officer suggested that production facilities be set up so that the company might manufacture its own requirements of this operating supply.

> The Carrigan Manufacturing Company . . . was considered a large user of this product. For several years, however, the finishing department had complained about the quality of buffing compound being purchased. Dissatisfaction was based on (a) lack of uniformity in the buffing compound which resulted in scratches during the process of finishing, the elimination of which required additional buffing, and (b) improper seasoning, which caused an excessive consumption of compound when the latter was too moist and excessive heat and dragging of the metal when too dry. Although buffing compounds represented but a small part of the company's annual purchases . . ., the purchasing officer was considerably concerned because his department had been unable to obtain a compound satisfactory to the finishing department. Furthermore,

although the actual expenditure for buffing compound constituted but a small part of the total manufacturing cost, the quality of the compound selected did have a substantial effect on the length of time required for finishing and therefore indirectly contributed to the cost of performing this operation.

. . . the laboratory of the Carrigan Manufacturing Company experimented with buffing compounds and successfully developed a formula that met the company's requirements. The laboratory's research work and trial production in small quantities indicated that the manufacturing process consisted simply of mixing the ingredients and storing them for a period of three months. It was apparent that the manufacturing cost would be small in relation to the raw material cost. The additional facilities needed by the company for producing its own compound would necessitate so small an expenditure as to be negligible. Moreover, the process of manufacturing required no technical skill.

. . . the direct expense incident to the company's manufacture of its own requirements would total about $7.00 per 100 pounds. Although there was no standardized price for buffing compounds, $8.00 per 100 pounds was approximately what the company would reasonably expect to pay for the compound if it continued to buy from outside concerns. In addition to the saving, manufacture of its own requirements would give the company complete control over quality.

There was an alternative method by which satisfactory quality could be obtained, however. The Carrigan Manufacturing Company might make arrangements with some supplier whereby the latter would (a) produce the compound in accordance with the Carrigan formula and (b) deliver the unseasoned product to the company's plant where aging would be under the company's control. Past experience had convinced the purchasing officer that suppliers could not be depended upon to carry sufficient inventory to ensure proper seasoning.[3]

In the above case, the purchasing officer of Carrigan checked with various sources to determine if buffing compounds of satisfactory quality could be obtained on the outside. It was determined they could not; however, they could be manufactured in-house. As the increase in direct costs was less than the purchase cost, the make alternative was selected.

The fact that no supplier makes the desired quality should be the cause of some concern because it may indicate that producers have not had requests for such a high degree of quality. Before the make option is chosen, the firm should make sure that it is capable of economically producing the desired quality in-house.

A further review of the quality specifications may indicate that they are unnecessarily high. If they were set more realistically, the buy alternative might be feasible. If a make alternative is still indicated, the firm should undertake a thorough investigation to determine if it can produce at the

---

[3] James W. Culliton, *Make or Buy,* Harvard University, Division of Business Research, Boston, Mass., 1961, pp. 34-35.

desired level of quality. In addition, consideration should be given as to whether a supplier's lack of desired quality is only a temporary situation.

In the case of a new product or process, or where the supplier's lack of desired quality will be temporary, rather than selecting an expensive make option, the firm might do the following and still select the buy alternative:

(1) redetermine desired quality with a view toward buying substitutes until the originally desired quality is offered by suppliers, or
(2) aiding suppliers in developing the desired quality.

These points should be considered extensively because once a decision to manufacture is executed, it can be changed only at great cost.

Better Control

Many firms feel that because the reputation of their business relies on the maintenance of desired quality standards, this maintenance is too important to be left to an outsider. The following case illustrates the make option taken to ensure a promotional policy:

> ...a manufacturer of an advertised line of baby furniture stressed the guarantee of its products. As a protective device, its written guarantee contained a clause excluding parts not of its own manufacture. It was discovered that the company was incurring much ill will because of the failure of the nonguaranteed parts manufactured by suppliers. As a consequence, the firm adopted a policy of making rather than buying in order to ensure its promotional policies.[4]

One may argue that rather than in-house production, quality standards can be maintained by rigid inspection of purchased items when received. However, it was pointed out during this study that the cost of testing and rejecting purchased items below standard may be so great that making might lead to lower inspection costs by combining inspection and quality control.

Another related argument that was made is that because the user better understands the intricacies connected with the usage of the part than does an outside supplier, there would be some advantage to him to manufacture it in-house. First of all, the user would be better able to coordinate quality considerations in the production of the part and its assembly. In addition, the combining of all operations in one plant would eliminate many communication problems which can arise between buyer and seller.

Favor Buying

Arguments based on quality that favor buying are that: the quality

---

[4]J. H. Westing, et. al., *Purchasing Management: Materials in Motion* (Chapter 13: Make or Buy), John Wiley & Sons, New York, 1976, p. 278.

cannot be made, a producer is more skillful, the purchaser has greater flexibility and the ability to take advantage of the vendor's continuing quality improvements.

Cannot Be Made

An obvious reason in favor of buying would be if an item of the desired quality could not be produced in-house. This situation happens most often because the item itself is patented or the production method is controlled by the supplier. In this case the only alternative would be to buy or to change specifications so that substitutes can be used.

Another reason why the desired quality cannot be made in-house is that the plant does not have the technical capability to meet the desired level. Although this capability may be obtained, the cost would be prohibitive.

Producer Is More Skillful

One of the most compelling reasons for buying is that a vendor probably is more skilled in producing one's regular line than the user of an item who produces it as a sideline. Thus, purchasing would take advantage of the supplier's specialization and probably result in obtaining items of better quality. In addition, due to this specialization and greater volume, the skillful producer would probably have cost advantages over a company producing the item as a sideline.

Flexibility

A firm that is purchasing has greater flexibility in adapting to any changes in the desired quality of the item. If a company has invested in production facilities to produce a part, it may be difficult and expensive to make changes in these facilities to alter production. On the other hand, if the item is being purchased, the firm has a flexibility to change the supplier as well as the type of product being bought.

Quality Improvements

The production specialist will undoubtedly continue to keep up with current developments in the field. Thus, buying will enable a firm to take advantage of a vendor's research and development and his ability to improve on quality. The purchaser can do this without increasing costs or risking loss of investment.

The ability to keep up with improvements in quality and greater flexibility, as indicated in the previous point, are important arguments in favor of buying in an industry that undergoes frequent technological changes.

Arguments Favor Buying

Based on this study, if everything is equal, it appears that arguments based on quality favor buying rather than making. The principal reasons for the above conclusion have been summarized as follows:

1. The experience of a specialized supplier in most cases is just as conducive to producing the desired quality as a company's own organization.
2. A purchaser benefits in the research activity of a progressive supplier and is, therefore, better able to maintain flexibility and to keep up with the times.
3. Buying avoids, for the purchaser, the costs of developing efficient production methods and processes or, in other words, the costs of becoming a specialist in manufacturing a product.[5]

Quantity

Unlike quality, which can be accurately determined and described, desired quantity changes with time and conditions. Thus, while desired quality is usually stable, the correct quantity is not. This section assesses the impact of quantity considerations on the make-or-buy decision.

Small Quantities

The need for small quantities can either favor making or buying. The following discusses the influence of excess capacity and economic order quantities on the decision to make or buy small quantities.

Excess Capacity

An important reason for making, from a quantity viewpoint, would be that the amount required is too small to interest a supplier except as a more expensive special order. In such instances, the firm may be able to utilize some of its excess capacity to meet these small orders. In his book *Make or Buy,* Culliton reports on a firm that met its small orders in this manner.

> The Lillis Company, a large manufacturer, had occasional demand for chairs and tables of an unusual design which could not be purchased except on special

---

[5] Kenneth F. Schuba, "Make-or-Buy Decisions—Cost and Non-Cost Considerations," *NAA Bulletin,* March 1960, pp. 61-62.

order. The company never needed many at any one time, so the costs on special order from furniture manufacturers were much higher than for standard chairs or tables. For its manufacturing business, the company had a woodworking shop principally engaged in making patterns. The woodworkers, however, possessed general skill and in their spare moments [produced] these chairs and tables. The men, therefore, had more steady work; the company's woodworking shop was more fully used; and the cost to the company for the furniture was less. In this case...the small quantities involved made it impossible for outside suppliers to meet the company's costs.[6]

Thus, if a supplier will not fill an order or it will be costly because it is too small, and excess capacity exists at the firm, the make alternative might be selected.

Economic Quantities

Before deciding to self-manufacture because no supplier is interested in producing the small quantities involved, the following interesting suggestion has been made:

...a (firm) should consider whether buying a sufficient quantity and carrying an inventory for a longer period of time may not be feasible. It should also consider whether it would be possible to change specifications so that several small-use items could be included under common specifications. Furthermore, it is vital that the implications of making a small-use item in one's own plant be considered. If it is unprofitable for a supplier to accept small-quantity orders, it may be equally unprofitable for the user to make them.[7]

The text, *Purchasing Management: Materials in Motion*, applies the Economic Order Quantity (EOQ) to the make alternative and discusses it in relation to the EOQ for purchasing. The following is based on that discussion.

The normal EOQ formula is:

$$EOQ = \sqrt{\frac{2AC}{B}}$$

where A = order costs
C = annual usage in volume
B = carrying charges

[6]Culliton, *op. cit.*, p. 52.
[7]Westing, *op. cit.*, pp. 279-280.

This can be adapted to the make decision as follows:

$$EOQ = \sqrt{\frac{2US}{ID}}$$

where U = expected usage in units over time
S = set-up costs or purchase costs (materials and supplies)
I = inventory carrying charge as a percentage (including value of money invested, insurance, and other overhead items)
D = cost per unit (direct manufacturing costs when in-plant production is involved)

The major differences in the formulas are that in the second: (1) order costs in the numerator are changed to set-up costs and (2) carrying charges in the denominator are broken down into inventory carrying charges and unit manufacturing costs.

The economic lot size of the make-or-purchase alternative assuming the following would be:

Annual Usage: 100 pieces
Purchase Price: $10
Cost to Make: $10

Manufactured Lot:
Carrying Charge—25%
Set-up Costs—$100

$$EOQ = \sqrt{\frac{2 \times 100 \times 100}{0.25 \times 10}}$$

$$EOQ = \quad 89$$

Purchased Lot:
Carrying Charge—25%
Purchase Costs—$10

$$EOQ = \sqrt{\frac{2 \times 100 \times 10}{0.25 \times 10}}$$

$$EOQ = \quad 28$$

44

Thus, the economic lot size for the manufacture option would be 89, while only 28 for the purchase option. Furthermore, as set-up costs increase, so does the disparity between the economic quantities for making versus purchasing. For this reason it often may be more economical to buy small quantities rather than produce them in-house.

Closer Coordination

A reason sometimes advanced for making based on quantity considerations is that the producing firm should be better able to coordinate the quantity produced and required. It is held that, because the firm has control over production scheduling, it can more readily change production of a finished part to meet shifts in forecasted demand for that part. This is particularly important where demand fluctuates and it is difficult to forecast requirements accurately.

There is some doubt whether this is a valid argument. In fact, one might argue that it is easier and cheaper to change the rate of purchases than to adjust the scheduling of a complex manufacturing process to meet changing demands. Thus, whether the desire for closer coordination between input and output favors making or buying probably depends on the complexity of the manufacturing process.

Large Quantities

As with small quantities, the need for large quantities may favor making *or* buying. If one supplier cannot produce the entire order of a firm because the order is too large, it would have to be split among several suppliers. Assuming the product had to be manufactured with special dies, it might be too costly to furnish each supplier with these dies. In such a case, the make alternative might be selected. On the other hand, the production of such a large quantity in-house might interfere with regular production and buying from several outside suppliers might be preferable.

Thus, each of the arguments presented here in reference to quantity can either favor making or buying, depending upon circumstances. The fact that quantity considerations usually are not too important in this decision is verified by the following quote:

> In summary, it seems that arguments based upon quantity are seldomly so important as to justify, in themselves, making rather than buying. In most instances, therefore, quantity becomes a supplementary argument to add to a list of other arguments....[8]

---

[8] Culliton, *op. cit.*, pp. 53-54.

Dependability of Supply

Dependability of supply is often an important consideration in make or buy. More than 63% of the respondents to the questionnaire indicated it was a very or extremely important consideration. Related to dependability of supply are procurement lead time and multiple sources, both of which will be discussed here.

Procurement Lead Time

One of the questions on the mail survey asked the relative influence of procurement lead time on this decision. Although 21.0% of the respondents disclosed that it was of no or little importance, 74.8% indicated that it was moderately or very important. Another 4.2% of the respondents claimed procurement lead time was an extremely important factor.

It was pointed out that a firm would generally reduce delays due to strike, natural disaster or transportation problems, and the like, if it produced its requirements in-house rather than purchasing from outside suppliers. However, as in-house production would seem to be subject also to many of these delays, the advantage of self-manufacturing would not seem to be that great.

Multiple Sources

If a firm purchased all the requirements of a particular item from one supplier, it would be extremely vulnerable if that supplier went out of business, significantly cut back production, or increased prices to an unreasonable level. Likewise, if all requirements were made in-house, the firm would be very vulnerable to work stoppages or other delays.

Particularly for costly or specialized parts or materials, a firm should have multiple sources of supply, thus spreading its risks. A portion of one's requirements might be produced in-house and the balance purchased from outside suppliers. In this way, the user will ensure a source of supply and have an effective weapon to help keep down the price of the vendor.

Less than 18% of the respondents to the questionnaire indicated that multiple sources was a very or extremely important consideration in this decision. In subsequent discussions it was commented that although a multiple source policy will spread risks, due to the loss of quantity discounts and because of the economies of scale, it usually proves more expensive. Thus, this increased cost must be weighed against the benefits the firm will derive from such a policy.

46

Chapter 5

Survey Results

The design of the mail survey was described in Chapter 1, while this chapter will contain an in-depth analysis of the results. The questionnaire is reproduced in Appendix A.

Formal Policy

The first question asked whether the firm had a formal or written make-or-buy policy. The responses were as follows:

	No.	Percent
Yes	39	31.5
No	85	68.5
	124	100.0

The chief purposes of this question were to disclose:

(1) how many firms considered this decision significant enough to be covered by a formal policy, and

(2) potential candidates for the interviews and development of case studies.

It was anticipated that the firm that had a formal policy would most probably make a better contribution to the remaining phases of the study than one that did not. Thus, those respondents who answered this question affirmatively were contacted to determine if they would participate further in the project. These contacts resulted in interviews being conducted at 18 U.S. and Canadian firms. The purpose of the interviews was to examine the decision process more carefully and to develop case studies.

As indicated in the above table, almost one-third of the firms have a formal or written policy. Upon further discussion with them, it became clear that this figure was too high. Most respondents in actuality were referring to their capital expenditure policy. They stated that this policy did not refer to make or buy, except that, if the decision to make required the acquisition of equipment, the capital expenditure policy would be followed. Thus, the follow-up research to this question confirms that the great majority of firms do not have a formal or written policy in this area.

Participants in Decision

The second question surveyed which departments or disciplines within the firm generally provide input into the make-or-buy decision. Preprinted on the questionnaire were seven disciplines which the respondent could check. They were: top management, manufacturing, engineering, purchasing, marketing, accounting, and labor relations. Space was also provided for other responses to be written in. The following table summarizes the frequency with which the preprinted disciplines were selected. The percentages were calculated by using total replies received (124) as the denominator. Their total is greater than 100% because in almost all cases respondents checked several disciplines as providing input.

	No.	% of 124
Manufacturing	105	84.7%
Accounting	91	73.4%
Purchasing	89	71.8%
Engineering	87	70.2%
Top Management	74	59.7%
Marketing	48	38.7%
Labor Relations	16	12.9%

As can be seen, the manufacturing department most often participates in the decision. A total of 105 or 84.7% of the respondents disclosed that manufacturing provides input. Somewhat surprisingly, the purchasing function ranked third—behind manufacturing and accounting. A little less than 72% of the respondents indicated that the purchasing function is a participant.

In deciding whether to manufacture an item or purchase it on the outside, one would think that the manufacturing and purchasing areas should be the chief participants. The fact that accounting seems to be more involved than purchasing might be explained in a couple of ways. First, because the mail survey was initially directed to the chief financial officer of the firm, the role of the accounting function might be somewhat overemphasized in the responses. Second, purchasing data such as purchase price could, and probably often does, come from accounting rather than purchasing, whereas, such information as the availability of capacity, the ability to meet certain standards of quality, and the like, would have to come from the manufacturing department.

A number of respondents wrote in additional areas in their replies. These areas and the number of participants who mentioned them were as follows:

	No.
Planning	5
Quality Control	3
R&D	3
Originating Department	2
Service Departments	1
District Operations	1
Supply and Coordination	1
Corporate Relations	1
Customers	1
Parts and Accessories Sales	1

It would seem reasonable to expect that planning, quality control and R&D participate in the decision more often than is indicated above. Probably other replies included these areas as part of the accounting and engineering departments.

From some of the replies, it became apparent that the participants would vary somewhat depending upon the dollar amount and type of product involved. A couple of respondents indicated that top management must participate if a large investment is required. Likewise, the marketing function, even if it did not normally provide input, would usually be involved in the decision to make or buy a brand-new product.

Primary Responsibility

The third question was designed to denote who within the firm has the primary responsibility to make this decision. It listed the same seven disciplines as the previous question, with the addition of an interdisciplinary committee. The responses are summarized on page 50. Of the 124 respondents, 85 checked one of the preprinted captions, four wrote in a response, and the remaining 35 indicated that several disciplines have primary responsibility.

As indicated in the table, the preprinted disciplines that were selected, in order of frequency, were: top management, interdisciplinary committee, manufacturing, accounting, purchasing, and engineering. No one selected marketing or labor relations.

	No.	Percent
Top Management	52	42.0
Interdisciplinary Committee	17	13.7
Manufacturing	9	7.3
Accounting	3	2.4
Purchasing	2	1.6
Engineering	2	1.6
Marketing	0	-0-
Labor Relations	0	-0-
Several Disciplines Checked	35	28.2
Others Written In	4	3.2
Total	124	100.0

All four written-in responses referred to lower levels of management. The first two indicated that department management had primary responsibility; the third, divisional management committee; and the fourth, department head of using department.

Initially the responses that had several disciplines checked caused some confusion. It was thought that perhaps they referred to an informal interdisciplinary committee. In the course of subsequent discussions with many of the respondents, however, it became apparent that this was not so. In these discussions, it was stated that instead of only one, several disciplines are collectively responsible for making this determination, and the participants vary with the type of decision.

The table on page 51 indicates the responses of the 35 participants who checked several disciplines. As few as two, and as many as six, of the disciplines were checked by participants. By far the areas that were indicated as sharing in the primary responsibility most often were manufacturing and top management. They were mentioned in 62.9% and 60% of the replies respectively. They were followed by purchasing, accounting, engineering, interdisciplinary committee, and marketing. The three responses that were written-in referred to lower levels of management (division management and the originating department).

From subsequent conversations, it became clear that top management's participation often was simply that it had to give final approval. Although this approval is often just a formality, it is required, particularly if the amounts involved are large. Likewise, manufacturing was included so often because it was indicated that only it can give the best assessment of whether an item can be made in-house.

One participant commented that manufacturing has primary responsibility on recommendation from purchasing. A couple of respondents, who checked manufacturing and other disciplines, indicated that manufacturing is primary.

ANALYSIS OF RESPONSES TO QUESTION 3 IN WHICH SEVERAL DISCIPLINES WERE CHECKED

DISCIPLINES

	A	B	C	D	E	F	G	H	OTHER
1		X	X	X	X	X	X		
2		X			X		X		
3			X		X				
4		X	X						
5			X	X	X				
6			X		X				
7	X	X							
8			X						DIVISION MGMT.
9		X	X						
10					X		X		
11				X	X				
12		X					X		
13	X								DIVISION MGMT.
14	X	X							
15			X	X					
16			X		X		X		
17			X	X	X		X		
18			X	X					
19		X	X						
20		X	X			X			
21	X	X							
22		X							ORIGIN. DEPT.
23	X	X					X		
24		X	X						
25		X	X	X	X	X			
26	X	X							
27		X			X				
28		X	X		X		X		
29		X	X						
30		X	X						
31			X				X		
32			X		X				
33	X	X							
34		X	X						
35			X	X					
Totals	7	21	22	8	13	3	9	-0-	
% of 35	20.0	60.0	62.9	22.9	37.1	8.6	25.7	-0-	

CODES FOR DISCIPLINES

A	Interdisciplinary Committee
B	Top Management
C	Manufacturing
D	Engineering
E	Purchasing
F	Marketing
G	Accounting
H	Labor Relations

As with other questions, the discipline that exercises primary responsibility could vary, depending upon the nature of the decision. For example, if it were imperative that the item to be manufactured in-house meet very rigid quality standards, the role of the engineering department, which might normally be minimal, could become primary.

One respondent indicated the manufacturing, purchasing and accounting departments each have primary responsibility for a different factor. They are: manufacturing—for technological competence; purchasing—for vendor assessment; and accounting—for economic evaluation.

Another respondent, who checked only top management as having primary responsibility, indicated that all areas share in making this decision. Included on this reply was the following comment:

> All functional areas contribute to make/buy decisions. Primary responsibility rests with top management who will make the decision after careful consideration of (1) the input from functional managers and (2) assessment of what is best for the business.

Impact of Various Factors

Question 4 assessed the impact of 12 considerations or factors on the make-or-buy decision. The respondents were asked to rate the relative importance of each in the decision process. The considerations were financial (cost, investment, and ROI) and nonfinancial (manufacturing capacity, employment stability, confidentiality of process, quality control, manufacturing expertise, dependability of supply, procurement lead time, multiple sources, and technological obsolescence).

The table on the following page contains an analysis of how each of these considerations was rated. It indicates the number of respondents who checked each factor's importance as being none, little, moderate, very or extreme. These were then totaled for each factor and a percentage to the total calculated.

As can be seen, of the 120 participants who rated the cost factor, 36 or 30% indicated that this factor was Extremely Important, 74 or 61.7% that it was Very Important, etc.

To assist in the interpretation of the results to this question, the following paragraphs simply list the degree of importance that the greatest number of (*most*) respondents selected for each factor. The only areas in which a clear majority (over 50%) exists were in the category Very Important for cost (61.7%), ROI (52.5%), and dependability of supply (53.8%).

The factors listed on page 54 were rated as being *Very Important* by *most* respondents.

ANALYSIS OF REPLIES TO QUESTION 4

FACTOR	TOTAL REPLIES		NONE		LITTLE		MODERATE		VERY		EXTREME	
	No.	%	No.	%	No.	%	No.	%	No.	%	No.	%
COST	120	100	0	-0-	1	0.8	9	7.5	74	61.7	36	30.0
INVESTMENT	118	100	1	0.8	9	7.6	24	20.4	57	48.3	27	22.9
ROI	120	100	2	1.7	6	5.0	11	9.1	63	52.5	38	31.7
MANUFACTURING CAPACITY	113	100	2	1.8	10	8.8	32	28.3	51	45.2	18	15.9
EMPLOYMENT STABILITY	115	100	5	4.3	42	36.5	48	41.8	16	13.9	4	3.5
CONFIDENTIALITY OF PROCESS	116	100	21	18.8	38	32.8	26	22.4	21	18.1	10	8.6
QUALITY CONTROL	118	100	4	3.4	17	14.4	39	33.1	47	39.8	11	9.3
MANUFACTURING EXPERTISE	117	100	2	1.7	13	11.1	40	34.2	56	47.9	6	5.1
DEPENDABILITY OF SUPPLY	117	100	4	3.4	7	6.0	32	27.4	63	53.8	11	9.4
PROCUREMENT LEAD TIME	119	100	3	2.5	22	18.5	53	44.5	36	30.3	5	4.2
MULTIPLE SOURCES	114	100	3	2.6	42	36.8	49	43.0	19	16.7	1	0.9
TECHNOLOGICAL OBSOLESCENCE	114	100	7	6.1	32	28.1	53	46.5	21	18.4	1	0.9

Cost
Investment
ROI
Manufacturing Capacity
Quality Control
Manufacturing Expertise
Dependability of Supply

The following factors were rated as being *Moderately Important* by *most* respondents:

Employment Stability
Procurement Lead Time
Multiple Sources
Technological Obsolescence

The following factor was rated as being of *Little Importance* by *most* respondents:

Confidentiality of Process

No factors were rated as being of *None* or *Extreme Importance* by most participants.

As indicated above, seven considerations were rated as being Very Important by *most* participants. To say that dependability of supply is *more important* than ROI simply because more respondents rated it as Very Important would be incorrect. This is obvious because 31.7% indicated ROI as Extremely Important, against only 9.4% for dependability of supply. Thus, ROI was rated by more participants as being either Very or Extremely Important.

In an attempt to rank the relative importance of each of the Very Important factors, the following will list, in order, the combined percentages of respondents that indicated each factor as either Very or Extremely Important.

Factor	Very + Extreme
Cost	91.7%
ROI	84.2%
Investment	71.2%
Dependability of Supply	63.2%
Manufacturing Capacity	61.1%
Manufacturing Expertise	53.0%
Quality Control	49.1%

This indicates that cost is the most important consideration. It was listed by 91.7% of the respondents as being either Very or Extremely Important (61.7% + 30.0%). Of second and third importance were the other two financial considerations—ROI and investment. It is interesting to note that dependability of supply was the most important nonfinancial consideration, followed by manufacturing capacity, manufacturing expertise, and quality control.

As with other questions on this survey, the importance of a factor would vary with a specific situation. This is particularly true of confidentiality of process. Although 50.9% (18.1% + 32.8%) indicated that this factor was of No or Little Importance, a rather high 26.7% (18.1% + 8.6%) indicated that it was Very or Extremely Important.

The importance of confidentiality would vary depending upon the product involved. For example, if the manufacturing process was a closely guarded secret, this factor would be of paramount importance and probably outweigh all others. In fact, a couple of respondents indicated that confidentiality was generally of little importance; however, whenever applicable, it was extreme.

This question also asked participants to write in other factors which are considered in their decision. They were:

> Degree of Risk of Product Failure
> Quality of Competition
> Product Life Where Component Will Be Consumed
> Environmental Impact
> Useful Life
> Maintenance
> Standardization
> Sales
> Full Costs
> Labor Relations
> Financial Capability

Cost and Time Value of Money

The fifth question was in two parts. It assessed the use of (a) full or marginal cost, and (b) the time value of money in the financial evaluation of this decision.

The first part of the question was designed to determine whether full or marginal costs are more predominantly used in the decision process. Although the literature debates this point extensively, the arguments are inconclusive. A large number of participants checked *both* full and marginal, and others included and checked a third caption—*BOTH*—on their reply.

Thus, the analysis below indicates three categories:

	No.	Percent
Full	54	43.6
Marginal	48	38.7
Both	22	17.7
Total	124	100.0

It is probable that had the caption Both been included on the questionnaire, the results would have been different. Several participants, who probably would have checked a Both category, most likely rather arbitrarily chose Full or Marginal and some indicated that their choice held for short- or long-term decisions only.

Thus, it would be misleading to say that full costs are used more often than are marginal costs, as the above analysis would indicate. A conclusion that *can* be drawn from this response is, however, that the use of either of these types of costs *varies with the time frame involved*. Over the short-term, marginal costs predominate, while in the case of long-term projects, full costs are more important.

The response to the second part of the question, dealing with the time value of money, is summarized below:

	No.	Percent
Yes	106	85.5
No	15	12.1
No Answer	3	2.4
Total	124	100.0

Although the vast majority of the respondents indicated that they do consider the time value of money in their decision process, as with many of the previous questions, the response probably varies with the project being considered. For example, if the decision did not require additional investment, the time value of money would probably be a minor consideration and ignored. However, if additional investment were required, this factor would grow in importance. The reason three participants did not answer the question was probably that it was inadvertently ignored as it was the only question on the last page.

Chapter 6

Summary and Recommendations

This last chapter will summarize the conduct of the study, compare actual practice to the normative model, and present some recommendations based on the research.

Summary

This study was designed to examine actual practices in the make-or-buy decision process. It is a part of the continuing Business Decision Models Project co-sponsored by the National Association of Accountants and the Society of Management Accountants of Canada. Research included a literature search, mail survey, interview and the development of case studies.

Although the make-buy decision can be an important determination of the financial health of a firm, this study indicates that it is usually not given adequate attention and is often made in a simplistic fashion. This decision is actually a rather complex process, which requires the consideration of a host of financial and nonfinancial factors. Many of these factors are difficult to assess and require subjective judgment and input from several departments.

Particularly if no capital expenditure is required, this decision is often made informally and by lower-level employees. If additional investment is required, the decision process is usually formalized and the firm's capital expenditures policy is followed. The discounted cash flow of the make and buy alternatives are calculated and the approval of top management is often required.

The groups most often indicated as *participating* in this decision, in descending order, are manufacturing, accounting, purchasing, engineering, top management, marketing and labor relations. Top management most often has *primary responsibility* to make this determination. It was followed by an interdisciplinary committee, manufacturing, accounting, purchasing and engineering.

Although cost is the usual starting point in a make-buy determination, nonfinancial factors are often more important considerations. The type of cost data used generally varies with the time frame of the decision. Marginal costs are most important for the short-term, while full costs predominate for long-term decisions. Likewise, the importance of nonfinancial factors varies with the type of decision.

In spite of the fact that a good deal of the literature and many participants agreed that future costs and conditions should be considered in the make-buy evaluation, this was seldom done in practice on a formal basis. There was general agreement that good management practice dictates that the typical make-or-buy decision process at a firm should be improved.

Practice Compared to Normative Model

The normative model for the Make-Buy Decision, which was contained in *Normative Models in Managerial Decision-Making,* is illustrated in Appendix B. This model takes into account all implicit (including opportunity) costs on a discounted cash flow basis. Particularly if the amounts involved are small and no additional facilities required, research into actual practice indicates that the financial evaluation for make or buy generally includes only current costs and often ignores the time value of money.

In those firms that do employ a discounting technique to determine a make-buy alternative which requires additional investment, the normative model in Appendix B rather accurately portrays actual practice. The firm's cost of capital is usually the discount rate for the calculation of present value. Normally, rather than determining the present value of making and of buying separately, only the savings to be realized from the make-or-buy option are discounted. These savings result from changes in the cost of purchases, raw materials, labor and the like. In addition, this model suggests that such items as revenue foregone by utilizing existing facilities should be considered as well in make-buy evaluations. In practice, this may be done intuitively, but seldom on a formal basis.

Recommendations

This section will contain general recommendations concerning a firm's make-or-buy decision.

Inasmuch as so many ever-changing factors influence this decision, no rigid formulas or rules of thumb can be applied to the make-buy process. In addition, due to different organizational structures and policies, this process must vary between firms and often within the same firm. Rather than construct a single model which might be used as a guide in making this decision, the author refers the reader to the flowcharts of typical make and buy suggestions at Stener Inc. contained in Appendix C. It should be noted

58

that these flowcharts are illustrative of the process at Stener Inc. and not of practice in general.

With a view toward improving this decision process, the following contains important elements that are relevant to a good make-buy determination.

1. Establishment of Goals

The initial phase of a make-or-buy study should be concerned with the establishment and/or recognition of the goals of the firm, as well as its resource and manufacturing capabilities and limitations. Each alternative should then be examined to determine if it is in compliance with these goals, capabilities or limitations.

2. Use of Interdisciplinary Committee

Because a proper make-buy study requires input from many sources, several departments in a firm must be involved in its execution. An interdisciplinary committee should have the primary responsibility for making this decision. This committee should include representatives from manufacturing, purchasing, accounting, marketing, engineering, and other departments that are affected by the decision.

3. Cost Considerations

The use of marginal costs is generally sufficient in a make-buy determination which is short-term in nature. For long-term decisions, particularly if the operational policy of the firm will be affected, full cost should be used in the analysis. In cases where the time frame of the decision is not clear, or where both the short-term and long-term effects of a decision are to be analyzed, *both* marginal and full costs should be calculated.

4. Nonfinancial Considerations

Nonfinancial considerations (quality, dependability of supply, workforce stability, and the like) must be carefully assessed for a possible influence in this decision. If considered important, the influence of these nonfinancial factors must be properly weighed, usually in a subjective manner. Although the importance of nonfinancial factors will vary from decision to decision, they can far outweigh financial considerations.

5. Cost-Reduction Tool

For maximum effectiveness, the make-or-buy decision should be an integral part of a firm's cost-reduction process. This decision should be assessed not only when a new product is introduced, but for all products on a continuing basis. Likewise, the availability of additional capacity, the increase in the price of a purchased item, and other such events should act as a signal to re-examine the make-buy alternative.

6. Continuously Reviewed

Because there are so many constantly changing factors that affect make-buy, it is important that this decision should be constantly subject to review. Due to changes in technology, demand, competition, and the like, a good decision may become a bad one in a very short time.

Appendix A

Questionnaire

National Association of Accountants  919 THIRD AVENUE
NEW YORK, N.Y. 10022
(212) 754-9700

January 15, 1979

Dear Sir:

The National Association of Accountants and the Society of Management
Accountants of Canada are co-sponsoring a continuing Business Decision
Models project. The purpose of this continuing project is to identify
and interpret managerial information needs through a systematic
examination of the decision-making process. To accomplish this, an
examination is being made of the procedures followed in performing
nine frequently encountered, higher-level, nonroutine decisions. The
subject of the current study is the Make-or-Buy question.

The decision of whether to manufacture an item internally or to
purchase it from an outside supplier can have a critical long-range
effect on a firm's operating characteristics, and it is often complex
due to the many variables involved. The current study is intended to
examine how industrial firms actually decide this important question.
This brief questionnaire is designed to determine an overview of the
Make-or-Buy decision process at your firm. It contains five short
questions, all of which can be answered by use of check marks.

The questionnaire is being mailed to a relatively small sample of
U.S. and Canadian firms. Therefore, your complete response is
earnestly solicited so that this study will make a meaningful contribution. Please have it answered by the individual best qualified
to do so. The preparer should sign it at the end and return it in
the enclosed self-addressed envelope.

The questionnaire is coded for follow-up purposes only. Individual
replies will be kept in strict confidence, and no companies will be
identified in the final report. The responses will be summarized and
reported in the aggregate. If you wish to receive a copy of the
results of this survey please indicate below the name and address it
should be mailed to:

_____

_____

_____

_____

If I can be of any further assistance, please contact me. Your
cooperation will be genuinely appreciated.

Sincerely,

Anthony Gambino
Research Associate

Appendix A

Questionnaire

1. Does your firm have a formal or written Make-or-Buy policy?
    _____ Yes
    _____ No

2. Which of the following areas within the firm generally provide input into your Make-or-Buy decision?
    _____ Top Management
    _____ Manufacturing
    _____ Engineering
    _____ Purchasing
    _____ Marketing
    _____ Accounting
    _____ Labor Relations
    Others (Specify)_____
    _____

3. Who has the primary responsibility to make this decision?
    _____ Interdisciplinary Committee
    _____ Top Management
    _____ Manufacturing
    _____ Engineering
    _____ Purchasing
    _____ Marketing
    _____ Accounting
    _____ Labor Relations
    Other (Specify) _____

4. By use of check marks, rate the relative importance (either none to extreme) of each of the following financial and nonfinancial considerations in your Make-or-Buy study.

	None	Little	Moderate	Very	Extreme
Cost	___	___	___	___	___
Investment	___	___	___	___	___
ROI	___	___	___	___	___
Manufacturing Capacity	___	___	___	___	___
Employment Stability	___	___	___	___	___
Confidentiality of Process	___	___	___	___	___
Quality Control	___	___	___	___	___
Manufacturing Expertise	___	___	___	___	___
Dependability of Supply	___	___	___	___	___
Procurement Lead Time	___	___	___	___	___
Multiple Sources	___	___	___	___	___
Technological Obsolescence	___	___	___	___	___
Others_____	___	___	___	___	___
_____	___	___	___	___	___
_____	___	___	___	___	___

5. In the financial evaluation of this decision, does your firm consider:
   (a) Full or only marginal costs?
      _____ Full
      _____ Marginal
   (b) The time value of money?
      _____ Yes
      _____ No

Please indicate below the name and title of the individual completing this questionnaire.

Name _____

Title _____

Appendix B

Normative Make-Buy Model

Appendix B

Normative Make-Buy Model*

Make-Buy Decision

Introduction

There are several methods of approach indicated in the literature for dealing with the make-buy decision. Among these, two techniques seem to be most popular. The first is to compare the estimated incremental operating costs of make or buy, where these costs are considered to remain constant over time. This approach usually does not consider the time value of money nor does it consider the implicit costs associated with the decision—e.g., opportunity costs related to the revenues foregone by utilizing existing plant facilities, costs associated with the need for larger inventories, and costs associated with the need for additional working capital.

The second technique, on the other hand, takes into account all incremental costs—e.g., operating costs, capital expenditures and implicit costs—on a discounted cash flow basis. Since this latter method generally is viewed as the theoretically correct approach, our model is of this type. See pages 68 and 69.

Elaboration on the Flowchart

1. *Make-Buy choice brought to the attention of management.* The make-buy choice situation is brought to the attention of management. It may take several forms. For example, the decision might be to make or buy a product the firm is not currently making or buying; it may be to *continue to make* or begin purchasing an item; or it may be to *continue to buy* or begin to

---

*(From Lawrence A. Gordon, et al., *Normative Models in Managerial Decision-Making*, National Association of Accountants, New York, and the Society of Management Accountants of Canada, Ontario, Canada, 1975, pp. 75-80.)

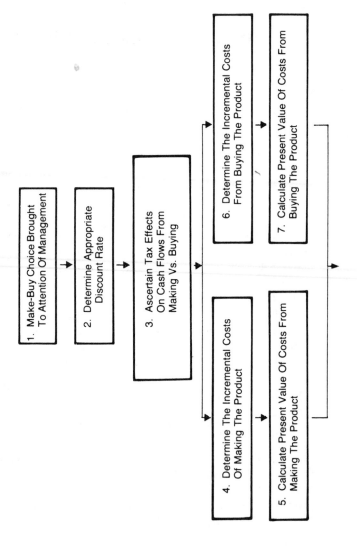

NORMATIVE MODEL OF MAKE-BUY DECISION

(DISCOUNTED CASH FLOW ANALYSIS)

1. Make-Buy Choice Brought To Attention Of Management

2. Determine Appropriate Discount Rate

3. Ascertain Tax Effects On Cash Flows From Making Vs. Buying

4. Determine The Incremental Costs Of Making The Product

5. Calculate Present Value Of Costs From Making The Product

6. Determine The Incremental Costs From Buying The Product

7. Calculate Present Value Of Costs From Buying The Product

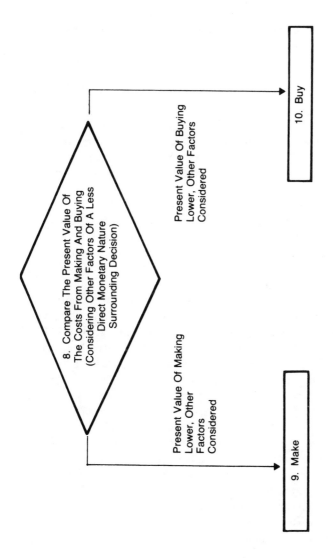

8. Compare The Present Value Of The Costs From Making And Buying (Considering Other Factors Of A Less Direct Monetary Nature Surrounding Decision)

Present Value Of Making Lower, Other Factors Considered

Present Value Of Buying Lower, Other Factors Considered

9. Make

10. Buy

manufacture an item. If the required capital investment to make the product is large, it is particularly important to view the decision as a capital budgeting decision in which discounted cash flows and opportunity costs of capital are considered. The present value (PV) method (see discussion on Capital Expenditure Decision) usually is advocated for this process.

2. *Determine appropriate discount rate.* When the discounted cash flow method is used for make-buy decisions, it is necessary to determine the appropriate discount rate for use in the discounting process. (See Capital Expenditure Decision, step 11, for a further discussion on determining the appropriate discount rate).

3. *Ascertain tax effects on cash flows from making vs. buying.* Taxes are a key, and often underemphasized, factor in comparing the merits of make and buy. For example, if the firm makes instead of buys a product, it must often buy plant and equipment in order to do so. These items result in depreciation which affects the cash outflows via the amount of taxes. Any other considerations which stem from tax regulations should be taken into account (e.g., the impact of early retirement due to obsolescence).

4. and 6. *Determine the incremental costs from making vs. buying.* If we assume that the selling price of the product is the same whether it is made or bought, the firm need look only at the costs of the make and buy alternatives. Examples of costs which may pertain specifically to the make alternative are investment in new equipment, revenues foregone by utilizing existing plant facilities, and incremental amounts of factory overhead (e.g., how would lighting, heating and indirect labor be affected). Costs which are important in looking at the buy decision include the costs associated with the additional inventories which may be required to be kept on hand to serve as a buffer. (This may not be necessitated under the make alternative where the firm has more control over the factors of production.) In summary, the key point is to consider all incremental costs for each alternative, including opportunity costs, for a number of periods into the future. (For a detailed list of those costs which are often important in the "make-or-buy" decision of manufacturing firms, see the NAA's MAP Statement No. 5, pp. 7-12.)

5. and 7. *Calculate the present value of costs from the make and buy alternatives.* An orderly way to set up this calculation is to take the number of periods deemed relevant to the project (often set equal to the expected economic life of the equipment to be purchased) and for each period estimate the costs, in terms of net cash outflows, pertaining to the project under each alternative. The net cash outflows, under each alternative, could be discounted using the following equation:

$$\text{Present Value} = \sum_{i=i}^{n} \frac{R_i}{(1+K)} i$$

where R is the net cash outflow for period i (which would consider any salvage value from capital investments made under the make alternative), K is the discount rate, and n is the number of periods under consideration.

8. *Compare the PV of the costs from making to that of buying.* If the PV of the costs of making is less than that of buying, then the direct monetary implication is that it will cost the company less to make the product than to buy it, and thus the product should be produced internally. Alternatively, if the PV of the costs of buying is less than that of making, then buying is cheaper and thus the preferred decision. However, nonfinancial factors which influence the make or buy alternative also must be examined. If the *make* alternative is cheaper, the analyst should examine whether there is much risk of equipment becoming obsolete. A firm could be severely prejudiced against the make alternative if high risk is considered to be present. The firm's areas of competence also may have to be examined to determine if the product to be produced can be manufactured and sold as a high quality item. Outside manufacturers might have more experience and may be prone to making a better product. Another factor which might negate the value of the make alternative would be the impact of making on the computation of financial ratios (e.g., the firm's ROI will be affected by the increased asset base where new facilities are needed to make the product). Some *value judgments* will have to be made to determine whether to go ahead with the chosen alternative or to re-evaluate the situation.

If the buy alternative appears better, again an examination of nonfinancial factors should be considered as a final selection exercise for determining the course of action to be taken. Some key factors which may enter the picture when the buy alternative is chosen are the foregone advantages of vertical integration, such as steady sources of supply and better control over product attributes. Also, if the firm decides to stop making the product, it must ascertain whether it could get rid of the excess manpower or allocate it effectively to other tasks without generating costly labor-management friction. (For further discussion on the nonfinancial consideration of the make-buy decision, the reader is referred to MAP Statement No. 5, pp. 15-18.)

9-10. These are action steps which follow from the analysis.

Appendix C
The Make-Buy Committee at Stener Inc.

The Make-Buy Committee at Stener Inc.

Stener Inc. is a large manufacturer in the household consumer goods industry. It has established a permanent Make/Buy Committee. This case will illustrate the working of that Committee and the flow of a typical make-or-buy decision at Stener.

Membership on this Committee is made up of representatives (a senior manager or director) from the following disciplines:

- Engineering
- Finance
- Scheduling
- Purchasing
- Value Engineering
- Inventory Control
- Manufacturing
- Manufacturing Methods

The purpose of this Committee is to coordinate the review of a make-or-buy decision. The operational guidelines of the Committee, as contained in Section III of its charter, are as follows:

A. A core member group will be established to initiate basic ideas and suggest products for review. This will constitute the permanent membership.

B. Appropriate parties will attend the MAKE/BUY meetings to participate in decisions and assignments affecting their operation. Subcommittees will be formed to bring about specific results. Major attention will be paid to bringing those concerned in at the inception of the specific ideas.

C. Selected COMMITTEE members will regularly visit other facilities to remain updated and aware of the outside world's capabilities.

D. MAKE and BUY products will be reviewed by performance specification rather than a "per print" basis to allow maximum benefits of

TYPICAL MAKE SUGGESTION FLOW

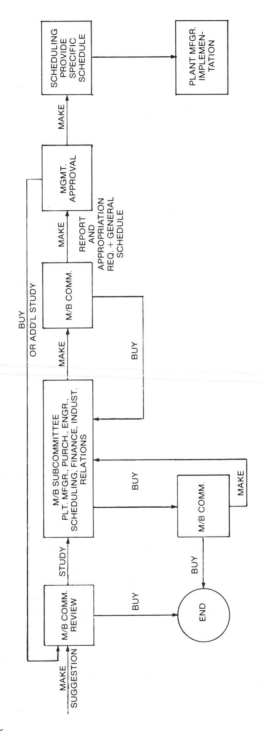

M/B COMM. = MAKE/BUY COMMITTEE

NOTE:

Subcommittee Will Provide

1. Capital Requirements
2. Product Make Cost (Per III-F)
3. True Purchased Cost
4. Impact on Labor Relations
5. Technology and Competitive Review

TYPICAL BUY SUGGESTION FLOW

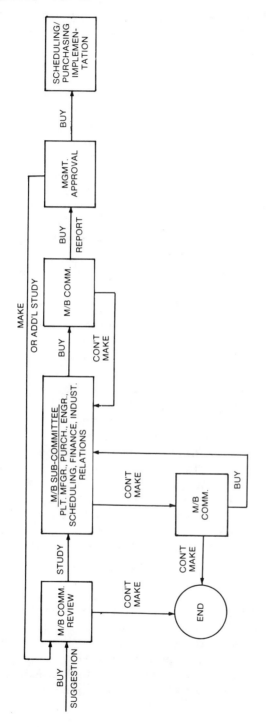

M/B COMM. = MAKE/BUY COMMITTEE

NOTE:

Where Product Is Internally Made the Following
Data Will be Provided by Subcommittee

1. Product Cost (Per III-F)
2. Improvement Potential
3. True Purchased Cost
4. Impact on Labor Relations
5. Technology and Competitive Review

77

inside and outside vendors' manufacturing potential and product design capabilities. Prints may be supplied for a starting point or guideline.

E. A competitive analysis system will be initiated. As products are reviewed they will be judged against what competition... has to offer. Understanding our position in relation to the rest of the world is an absolute requirement.

F. Costing will be presented in these forms—variable cost, variable cost plus incremental fixed, and a full cost base which includes the aforementioned plus facilities and management assessments. The cost of money, equipment amortization, raw material inventories, packaging, and transportation will be presented. Additionally, logistics and systems advantages will be detailed sufficiently so that they may be traded against any initially apparent higher cost or other penalties.

G. Vendor costing will be analyzed to gain a full understanding of how a MAKE candidate compares. This will provide a methods and materials comparison which will allow the best business decision, further proper costing and allow for long-term commitments.

H. All make decisions will be accompanied by a phase-in schedule.

The two flowcharts on pages 76 and 77 indicate the flow of a typical make suggestion as well as a typical buy suggestion at Stener. Since they are basically the same except for the last few steps, the following will discuss both flowcharts together.

The initial suggestion to make or buy might come from anywhere in the firm, including the Make/Buy Committee. The Committee will review the proposal and decide whether or not it should be studied further. If additional study is warranted, a Make/Buy Subcommittee will be formed to conduct this study. The disciplines that are represented on this Subcommittee are indicated in a box in each flowchart. They are plant manufacturing, purchasing, engineering, scheduling, finance, and industrial relations. Specific members vary depending on the type of product involved.

The data to be supplied by this Subcommittee are included as a note on each flowchart. Cost information is prepared in accordance with Section III. F. of the Make/Buy Committee Charter. This section indicates that three types of costs should be presented—variable, variable plus incremental fixed, and full cost.

The decision of the Make/Buy Subcommittee is then reviewed by the Make/Buy Committee. If they concur with the original suggestion to make or to buy, a report is submitted to management for final approval. In addition to the report, if the make alternative is being proposed, an Appropriation Request and General Schedule are also submitted.

The Appropriation Request is prepared for any new facilities needed to manufacture the product. It represents a request for the necessary capital expenditures. In order to evaluate the project, indicated on this form is the project's incremental effect on annual profit, payback period, and rate of return. The General Schedule indicates the time phasing of the project (e.g., when facilities will be acquired and production will begin).

After a project receives management approval, it then goes to the Scheduling Review Committee for action. Included on this Committee are representatives from manufacturing, purchasing, finance, engineering, scheduling, and parts sales. This Committee is responsible for implementation of the plan to buy. In the case of a make decision, the Scheduling Committee is responsible for providing specific schedules (e.g., inventory levels and production requirements) to ensure that the operations of Stener are not adversely affected. The plant manager of the manufacturing facility is charged with the actual implementation of the make plan.

Appendix D

Make-Buy in a Government Contract Bid

Make-Buy in a Government Contract Bid

Abco Corp. is an international company that is involved in the aerospace industry. A large portion of its work is done under government contract. In preparing a bid proposal for a contract, Abco must comply with the Armed Services Procurement Regulations (ASPR). One of the sections of ASPR requires a firm to conduct make-or-buy studies for different components of the contract. This case will discuss the Make-or-Buy Plan of Abco included in its bid on a large space program referred to as "The Project." It will illustrate how this decision is made in a case where nonfinancial factors were most important.

ASPR Regulations

ASPR mandates that a make-or-buy program must be included for those items of a contract which would normally require a make-or-buy review by company management due to their complexity, quantity, or cost, or because their production requires additional facilities. As a general guide, ASPR indicates that a make-or-buy program should not include those items of work effort costing less than 1% of the contract price or $500,000, whichever is less.

ASPR contains detailed procedures as to how the make-or-buy studies are to be performed. The following is taken from a portion of that procedure:

When submission of information with respect to a prospective contractor's proposed make-or-buy program is required, the solicitation shall so state and shall clearly set forth any special factors to be used in evaluating the program. After considering such factors as capability, capacity, availability of small business and labor surplus area concerns as subcontract sources, the establishment of new facilities in or near sections of concentrated unemployment or underemployment, contract schedules, integration control, proprietary processes, technical superiority or exclusiveness, and technical risks involved, the prospective contractor shall identify in his proposed make-or-buy program that work which he considers he or his affiliates, subsidiaries or divisions (i) must perform as "must make," (ii) must subcontract as "must buy," and (iii) can either perform or acquire by subcontract as "can make or buy." The prospective contractor shall state the reasons for his recommendations of "must make" or "must buy" in sufficient detail for the contracting officer to determine that sound business and technical judgment has been applied to each major element of the program.

It is interesting to note that, in addition to the usual concerns of capability, proprietary processes, etc., this regulation specifies that considerations should include the alleviation of unemployment and the utilization of small businesses as subcontractors.

Make-or-Buy Plan

In compliance with the above regulation, included in Abco's bid proposal for "The Project" is a detailed Make-or-Buy Plan. This Plan is discussed in the following pages.

The principal goals of Abco's Make-or-Buy Plan are to:

...develop optimum competition through maximum use of industrial resources, assure wide distribution of subcontract dollars, and provide flexibility of overall program operations to promote efficiency, establish the most cost-effective sources for each item, and assure maximum use of technology from NASA and other programs.

To provide for these goals, the following were the principal objectives of this Plan:

- Provide flexibility in overall program operations necessary to promote efficiency and to provide the most cost-effective source for each item.
- Maximize subcontract dollar distribution consistent with program economy and technical and business management control.
- Optimize competition and use of technological resources throughout the United States.
- Assure retention of desired capabilities required to support the programs through all phases.
- Provide for a manageable mix of in-house versus subcontract effort.
- Exercise appropriate control over critical systems and interfaces of "The Project."
- Maintain and assure make-versus-buy decisions result in competitive (viz., economical) total program cost and schedule position.
- To make maximum use of existing facilities, whether private or government owned, and thus minimizing or eliminating any new facility needs.
- That the greatest possible use is made of the knowledge gained from government technology contracts and other similar programs to obtain a maximum return on previous government investments.

In reaching make-or-buy determinations, all facilities, personnel, engineering, and production resources were evaluated in terms of program product quality, schedule, and cost objectives. Potential subcontractors were identified and proposals solicited in certain cases. The investments made by NASA and various corporations in the development of items during a related space project already completed were considered. In addition, the severable nature of the subsystem (i.e., its ease of interface and transportation) was assessed so as to minimize technical, schedule, and cost risks.

Make-or-buy decisions for "The Project" evolved through a series of reviews by a subcommittee management team consisting of key program engineering, manufacturing, facilities, and subcontracting (purchasing) personnel. As "The Project" configuration evolved, engineering prepared a listing of all the significant items (either by cost, schedule or both) by Work Breakdown Structure (WBS) element within the proposed configuration. This listing was the basis for all subsequent planning activity, identifying the system and subsystem nomenclature, the quantities required for the total program, and part numbers as they were developed.

To assure achievement of the objectives of the Make-or-Buy Plan, the subcontract management team developed specific criteria and applied them to "The Project." These criteria are illustrated in the following checklist. This checklist was used as a guide in evaluating hardware line items to determine the appropriate make-or-buy recommendations.

Checklist of Make-or-Buy Criteria

WBS_____

Description _____

Criteria	**Comments**

Capability

Design capability

Manufacturing capability

Production experience

Superior industrial
technology availability

Product of normal division
operation

Capacity

Engineering resources
available for design

Resources for managing
critical interface
requirements

Criteria	Comments

Criteria   **Comments**

Manufacturing personnel
available for production

Manufacturing facilities
available

New manufacturing facilities
required

Testing facilities available

New testing facilities
required

Transportation and movement
feasibility

Cost

Lowest cost decision

Optimum manpower levels

Cost control & visibility
mechanisms available

Transportation cost and
risk

Schedule

Support position of subsystem
to master program schedule

Transportation considerations

Technical Complexity

Configuration and manufacturing
control system for specialized
production articles

Early definition of procurement
requirements consistent with
engineering buildup

Criticality to program

Interface requirements control

Small Business & Labor Surplus

Small business participation
capability

Industrial capability in
designated labor surplus
areas

Criteria	Comments

Design and manufacturing
capability of minority-owned businesses

Basic Right of Industry to Compete

Established industry capability
or development

"State-of-the-Arts" advancement

Utilization of off-the-shelf
already developed items

Technical complexity level

Proprietary Rights

Are any of the required design
approaches or manufacturing
processes subject to established
proprietary rights?

Management Control

Manageability of change activity

Are there critical subsystems
interfaces which make it
impractical to subcontract?

Does Abco's build plan provide
for impractical Abco installation
after delivery of product?

Can the item be substantially
defined to permit proper cost
control and schedule for
subcontractor development?

One of the purposes of this checklist is to ensure that the ASPR regulations are followed. This is particularly evident in the section *Small Business and Labor Surplus*.

Each point in the above checklist was examined for all items in the Work Breakdown Structure (WBS). The effect of each criterion on the make-or-buy alternative was indicated in the comments section.

It should be noted that cost considerations are not the most important factors. Although this is often the situation in a make-or-buy decision, cost is even of less importance in this case. This is true because "The Project" is highly complex and requires critical interfacing.

Let us assume that Abco did not have adequate facilities to produce a specific item in-house. Rather than invest in these facilities, it would most probably be more economical to purchase it. Assuming that this item is severable from the rest of the project and subcontractors have experience in producing it, a buy decision would probably be made. On the other hand, if this item were not severable due to critical interfacing, it might be made in-house despite cost considerations.

After the previously discussed subcontract management team assesses the alternatives in the Make-or-Buy Plan, a formal *Make-or-Buy Committee* studies this Plan and makes its recommendations. This Committee is made up of divisional personnel and is usually chaired by a representative from the purchasing department. Other participants include representatives from manufacturing, quality control, industrial engineering, design engineering, and contract administration.

Final decisions are made by a formal *Make-or-Buy Board*. The Board is composed of the top management of the division (the President and those who report directly to him). The Chairman of the *Make-or-Buy Committee* is also a member of the *Board*.

Results of the Decision

The recommended make-or-buy decisions were presented in a series of charts in the bid proposal. Each WBS item is identified by nomenclature and appropriate designation; in addition, the major project elements are illustrated. Also provided for each item is a technical description along with the make-or-buy rationale.

Potential subcontractors for each buy item are shown as well as the subcontract start time after prime contract authorization is received. To further enhance visibility for each buy item, its approximate value has been provided. Proposals have been solicited from those firms designated with an asterisk. Proposals were not requested from the other firms because they are in competition with Abco for "The Project."

Chiefly to illustrate Abco's Make-or-Buy rationale for the various items, sections of the charts referred to are reproduced on the following pages. To maintain confidentiality, the illustrations and technical descriptions have been deleted. Furthermore, the names of potential subcontractors are fictitious.

The first four decisions indicate a buy alternative, while the next three a make decision. The chief rationale to buy included lack of experience or manufacturing capability at Abco, severability, and subcontractor know-how. The chief rationale for the make alternative were critical interfacing needs and the existence of manufacturing facilities and skills at Abco.

Nomenclature and WBS Identification	Technical Description	Make-or-Buy Decision Rationale	Potential Subcontractors	Approximate Value (in millions)			
				1 to 9	10 to 19	20 to 99	100
Environmental control, 2.3.5.1, 2. 3.5.2, 2.3.5.3		Buy — The noted corporations along with NASA and other agencies have invested in development and production of similar systems. This, coupled with the absence of an integrated design and manufacturing capability at Abco, along with competitive and economic considerations and an excellent record of subcontractor performance, establishes this as a buy item.	Helix* Bremo			X	
Food management 2.3.5.2		Buy — Abco has little experience with respect to this type of hardware, the hardware is well within the state of the art and excellent subcontractor capability is available from the firms noted.	Westco* Temden* Cresk*	X			
Radiator 2.3.5.3		Buy — This system, although scaled up, represents a derivative from a related project. The subcontractor noted has a strong know-how with respect to this item. It is severable; hence, in the interest of economy it will be bought.	Gristen*		X		

89

Nomenclature and WBS Identification	Technical Description	Make-or-Buy Decision Rationale	Potential Subcontractors	Approximate Value (in millions)			
				1 to 9	10 to 19	20 to 99	100
External LH$_2$/LO$_2$ tank 2.3.7		Buy — Although Abco has excellent experience in producing a tank of this type by virtue of its similarity to a related project, engineering buildup to perform detailed tank design, coupled with a most excellent subcontractor capability for this type of work, warrants considering this as a buy item. Moreover, the tank is severable from an interface standpoint as well as technically and administratively manageable. Furthermore, to make this tank competitively available to the industry serves to maximize distribution of "The Project's" economic impact throughout the country and maximizes the domestic technological base. (Subcontract to go-ahead ten months after prime ATP.)	Candit Temden* Gristen* Cresk*				X
Forward fuselage 2.3.1.1.		Make — Because of fairly critical interface between this orbiter element and the crew module, coupled with the objective of responding in a timely manner to subsystem changes and appropriate usage of qualified capabilities, skills and manufacturing facilities, a make decision is indicated.	not applicable	not applicable			

Nomenclature and WBS Identification	Technical Description	Make-or-Buy Decision Rationale	Potential Subcontractors	Approximate Value (in millions)		
				1 to 9	10 to 19	20 to 99 / 100
AFT fuselage 2.3.1.1.		*Make* — The orbiter-element features high-density packaging, considerable subsystem interfacing, and high criticality in relation to the overall vehicle. These facts, in light of experience accumulated by Abco on similar major structures, warrants a make decision.	not applicable	not applicable		
Final assembly, systems, installation and checkout 2.3.8		*Make* — By Abco accomplishing this work, maximum use of qualified experience in relation to capabilities, skills and activities will occur. Moreover, it will enhance timely response to subsystems change and will substantially satisfy the cost-effective objectives identified for the program. It also puts to use existing facilities.	not applicable	not applicable		

Appendix E

Make-Buy as a Continuous Decision

Make-Buy as a Continuous Decision

Melten Inc. is a major manufacturer in the pharmaceutical industry. Often in the production of a new product, or where it lacks capacity or the necessary expertise, Melten will have an outside contractor do the manufacturing. In such cases, it supplies the materials to the subcontractor, or vendor, who produces according to Melten's requirements. To ensure that high quality is maintained, Melten will rigidly inspect the final product and reject those items deemed inferior.

Project management is continuously involved in the evaluation of product profitability. One area that is investigated often is whether it would be cheaper to continue to manufacture an item in-house or have a subcontractor do it. The question of whether to continue subcontracting a job is usually raised at the time of a price increase or when excess in-house capacity becomes available.

Such an evaluation requires a formal make-or-buy study. This case will illustrate such a study to determine whether to continue to subcontract the manufacturing of the Finished Product Q or bring it in-house. For proprietary reasons the product name, quantities, ingredients and the like are fictitious.

Cost Sheets

Two Planning Analysis Cost Sheets are prepared. The first accumulates the costs of manufacturing Product Q in-house; the second updates the costs to produce at the subcontractor. Both are reproduced on the following pages and indicate the costs for 1,000 units of Product Q.

Each is prepared in current dollars and includes only variable expenses. Thus the in-house sheet contains the delivered cost of materials to Melten's plant, direct labor, and the variable burden applicable to the manufacture of Product Q.

The subcontractor, or vendor, cost sheet includes the delivered cost of materials to the subcontractor's plant, plus the vendor's charge. The mate-

IN-HOUSE MANUFACTURING

PLANNING ANALYSIS AND COST SHEET   DIVISION _____   EFFECTIVE DATE _____

MATERIAL OR OPERATION	CODE	Quantity Required	S T D	Standard Usage	U N I T	MATERIAL PRICE	MATERIAL COST	LABOR RATE	LABOR COST	VARIABLE BURDEN RATE	VARIABLE BURDEN COST	Total Variable Cost	ALLOCATED BURDEN OTHER RATE	OTHER COST	MILL RATE	MILL COST
RAW MATERIAL A	1111	250	100	27.5	lbs.	1980.0	544.50					544.50				
RAW MATERIAL B	2222	150.0	100	165.0	lbs.	2400.0	38600					38600				
RAW MATERIAL C	3333	175.0	100	192.5	lbs.	4900.0	943.25					943.25				
RAW MATERIAL D	4444	50.0	100	55.0	gal.	25900	1422.5					1422.5				
RAW MATERIAL E	5555	100.0	100	110.0	lbs.	7900.0	814.00					814.00				
PACKAGING F	6666	1200.0	50	1260.0	ea.	490.0	617400					617.00				
PACKAGING G	7777	1000.0	50	1050.0	ea.	2250.0	236.25					236.25				
LABOR	X	1000.0		1000.0	doz.				200.00			2000.00				
VARIABLE BURDEN	X	1000.0		1000.0	doz.						350.00	350.00				

PRODUCT FINISHED PRODUCT Q

COST QUAN. 1000 UNIT doz	UNIT COST TOTAL	9270.00 / 9.270	200.00 / .200	350.00 / .350	9820.00 / 9.820
SEE OR PUT-UP	UNIT COST TRANS.		

PACKING

VOLUME

TOTAL UNIT COST – Including Allocated Burden

DEPT. NO. _____ PAGE ___ OF ___ PRODUCT CODE _____

PLANNING ANALYSIS AND COST SHEET

DIVISION _____ EFFECTIVE DATE _____

| MATERIAL OR OPERATION | | Quantity Required | B/T % | Standard Usage | U/M | MATERIAL | | LABOR | | VARIABLE BURDEN | | Total Variable Cost | ALLOCATED BURDEN | | | |
DESCRIPTION	CODE					PRICE	COST	RATE	COST	RATE	COST		OTHER RATE	COST	MILL RATE	COST
RAW MATERIAL A	1111	25.0	100	22.5	lbs	.2000	55000					550.00				
RAW MATERIAL B	2222	150.0	100	165.0	lbs	.2500	4125					412.50				
RAW MATERIAL C	3333	175.0	110	192.5	lbs	.5000	96250					962.50				
RAW MATERIAL D	4444	500.0	110	550.0	gal	.3000	16500					165.00				
RAW MATERIAL E	5555	100.0	110	110.0	lbs	.7500	825.00					825.00				
PACKAGING F	6666	12000.0	100	12000.0	ea	.5000/0000.0	6300.00					6300.00				
PACKAGING G	7777	1000.0	100	1000.0	ea	.2500	262.50					262.50				
VENDOR CHARGE	X	1000.0	0	1000.0	doz	1500.0/1500.00	1500.00					1500.00				

PRODUCT FINISHED PRODUCT			1000	UNIT doz	Q		10,977.50					10,977.50				
COST QUAN.	1000	UNIT COST TOTAL			10.978							10.978				
SIZE OF...		UNIT COST TRANS.														
PACKING:																
VOLUME:																

TOTAL UNIT COST – Including Allocated Burden

DEPT. NO. _____ PAGE _____ OF _____ PRODUCT CODE _____

rials are supplied by Melten, whereas labor and overhead are absorbed by the subcontractor.

The in-house manufacturing cost sheet is prepared by the divisional accounting group. The bulk of the information comes from data supplied by manufacturing and engineering. They decide on the type of equipment, manning, efficiencies (waste %), and the like for in-house manufacturing. The cost of the materials, which includes freight, is supplied by the purchasing department. The labor cost is determined from manufacturing's estimates, and the variable burden is generally a percent of labor.

The subcontractor sheet is prepared by the purchasing department. In this instance, since Product Q is currently being manufactured at a subcontractor, purchasing simply updated the cost sheet that was previously prepared.

The in-house and subcontractor cost sheets will usually vary in some respects. For one thing, the standard usages and waste percentages on each sheet may be different since the subcontractor would ordinarily have greater experience in manufacturing the item. Likewise due to the differences in freight to the subcontractor's or to Melten's plant, the materials price would be different. In this case, because there is a savings in the freight of raw materials if the items were manufactured at Melten's, the material price on the in-house manufacturing sheet is less. In addition, instead of having a charge for labor and variable burden, the subcontractor's sheet includes a vendor charge. This is the subcontractor's reimbursement for his labor and overhead as well as profit.

Savings

As indicated, the variable costs of manufacturing Product Q in-house would be $9,820.25 for 1,000 dozen or a unit cost of $9.820/dozen. Because the cost of subcontracting is $10.978/dozen, the make alternative would save $1.158/dozen. In addition, if Product Q is manufactured at Melten's plant, there would be a substantial savings in freight payments for the shipment of *finished* goods to customers.

The marketing division supplied estimates of the quantities of Product Q that would have to be manufactured for the next 10 years to meet sales requirements. Those estimates are as follows:

Year	Volume in Doz	Year	Volume in Doz
1	–	6	87,219
2	55,268	7	92,401
3	72,539	8	97,582
4	77,720	9	102,763
5	83,765	10	108,808

Because in-house production is not expected to begin until the second year, the first year's volume is not included. It should be noted that it is anticipated volume will increase substantially. By the tenth year, it will practically double.

As indicated, in-house production will result in a reduction in variable cost and finished goods freight. Based on the above volume, plus a decrease in variable manufacturing costs of $1.158/dozen and a factor for finished goods freight reduction, the following yearly savings would result if the make alternative were selected:

Year	Variable Cost Savings	F.G. Freight Savings	Total Savings
1	-	-	-
2	$ 64,000	$32,000	$ 96,000
3	84,000	42,000	126,000
4	90,000	45,000	135,000
5	97,000	48,000	145,000
6	101,000	51,000	152,000
7	107,000	54,000	161,000
8	113,000	57,000	170,000
9	119,000	60,000	179,000
10	126,000	63,000	189,000

It should be noted that these savings ignore the effect of fixed costs and reflect current rather than future costs. As noted in this report, there is a continuing debate on the treatment of fixed and future costs in a make-buy analysis.

ROI

In order to bring Product Q in-house, the following investment costs would have to be incurred:

	Capital	Appropriation Expense
Equipment A	20,000	
Equipment B	35,000	
Miscellaneous	11,000	7,000
TOTAL	66,000	7,000

Appropriation expenses are those expenditures which cannot be capitalized but must be written-off immediately. Thus a decision to make would require the acquisition of $66,000 depreciable assets.

Standard Discounted Cash Flow Analysis
(000's Omitted)
Make vs. Buy - OOP ROI

	Year 1	Year 2	Year 3	Year 4	Year 5	Year 6	Year 7	Year 8	Year 9	Year 10
Variable Cost Savings		$ 64	$ 84	$ 90	$ 97	$ 101	$ 107	$ 113	$ 119	$ 126
F.G. Freight Savings		32	42	45	48	51	54	57	60	63
Other Savings										
Total MGF Savings		96	126	135	145	152	161	170	179	189
Depreciation	6	12	11	10	8	7	5	4	2	1
Appropriation Expense	7									
Engineering Expense										
Maintenance Expense										
Start-Up Costs	15									
Other Expense										
Total Expense	28	12	11	10	8	7	5	4	2	1
Operating P.B.T.	-28	84	115	125	137	145	156	166	177	188
Tax	-15	43	59	64	70	74	79	85	91	96
Investment Credit	7									
Operating P.A.T.	-6	41	56	61	67	71	77	81	86	92
Depreciation Addback	6	12	11	10	8	7	5	4	2	1
Total Cash In	0	53	67	71	75	78	82	85	88	93
M&E-3-Yr. Life										
M&E-7-Yr. Life										
M&E-9-Yr. Life										
Building & Building Eqp.	66									
Change in Working Capital										
Total Cash Out	66									
Net Cash Flow	-66	53	67	71	75	78	82	85	88	93
Cumulative Cash Flow	-66	-13	54	125	200	278	360	445	533	626

Present Value at Rate 15% 247

Value of Return on Investment 65.92%

The previous page contains a Discounted Cash Flow Analysis of the results of the decision to manufacture in-house. It calculates OOP (out-of-pocket) ROI.

Savings in variable cost and finished goods freight, discussed above, are recorded as manufacturing savings. Expenses will be increased by the accelerated depreciation of the $66,000 investment and the incurrence of appropriation expenses and startup costs.

In every year, except the first, the effect of a make alternative will be favorable on profit and net cash flow. In fact, over 10 years, cash flow will increase $626,000. At the firm's cutoff rate of 15%, the make alternative has a present value of $247,000. The discounted cash flow ROI is 65.92%. Based on cost considerations, the make alternative would seem extremely attractive.

Outcome

The upper management level of the division then considered the financial evaluation in conjunction with non-cost factors. Since much of Melten's manufacturing is continually done by subcontractors, the effect of bringing an item in-house on relations with these subcontractors is a non-cost consideration that has great weight.

Since it was deemed that vendor relations would not be hurt and after considering other non-cost factors, such as the availability of capacity, it was decided that Product Q should be made at Melten's plant. An appropriation request was prepared and formally approved by Corporate Management. A blank Appropriation Request Summary and Request Support used at Melten are included on the following pages.

102

APPROPRIATION REQUEST SUMMARY

COMPANY NAME	PROJECT TITLE	PROJECT CLASSIFICATION	DATE SUBMITTED

SUMMARY FINANCIAL DATA

(U. S. DOLLARS IN THOUSANDS)	AMOUNT REQUESTED	AMOUNT PROVIDED IN FORECAST			
		YEAR ___	YEAR ___	YEAR ___	YEAR ___
FIXED ASSETS					
PROJECT EXPENSE					
CONTINGENCY					
APPROPRIATION REQUEST TOTAL					
NEW WORKING CAPITAL					
TOTAL					

ECONOMIC LIFE ___ YEARS

AVERAGE RETURN ON INVESTMENT ___ %

PEAK CASH REQUIREMENTS	QUARTER	YEAR

CASH FLOW RECOVERY					
	1ST YEAR	2ND YEAR	3RD YEAR	4TH YEAR	5TH YEAR
	___ %	___ %	___ %	___ %	___ %

CASH PAY BACK: ___ YEARS

PROPOSED SOURCE OF FUNDS:

PROJECT DESCRIPTION

REASON FOR UNDERTAKING PROJECT

DATE TO START

ESTIMATED COMPLETION DATE

APPROVALS

NAME	DATE	NAME	DATE
NAME	DATE	NAME	DATE

APPROPRIATION REQUEST SUPPORT

PROJECT CLASSIFICATION

- ☐ Capacity Needed to Meet Forecasted Sales of Existing Products
- ☐ Accomodating New Products or Improvements of Existing Products
- ☐ Cost Reduction
- ☐ Replacement of Worn-Out Facilities
- ☐ Administration
- ☐ Research

COMPANY NAME
PROJECT TITLE
DATE SUBMITTED

A. CAPITAL RELATED CASH OUTLAYS	U.S. DOLLARS IN THOUSANDS					1ST 5 YR. TOTAL	REMAINING LIFE	TOTAL PROJECT
	19	19	19	19	19			
1. Fixed Assets:								
2. Land & Land Improvements								
3. Building & Building Equipment								
4. Machinery & Equipment								
5. Leasehold Improvements								
6. Total Fixed Assets								
7. Project Related Expense:								
8. New Project Expense								
9. Start-Up Costs								
10. Dismantling Costs								
11. Less: Salvage Value								
12. Total Project Expense								
13. Contingency								
14. Total Fixed Capital & Project Expense								
15. Working Capital Requirements								
16. Receivables								
17. Inventories								
18. Other								
19. Total Working Capital								
20. Total Capital Related Cash Outlays								

B. INCOME GENERATED

	U.S. DOLLARS IN THOUSANDS						1ST 5 YR. TOTAL	REMAINING LIFE	TOTAL PROJECT
	19	19	19	19	19	19			
21. Net Sales									
22. Direct Costs:									
23. Variable Mfg. & Distribution									
24. Depreciation									
25. Other Direct Cost of Sales									
26. Operating Expenses									
27. Interest Expense									
28. Plus: Project Expense									
29. Less: Cost Reduction									
30. DIRECT PROFIT CONTRIBUTION									
31. % to Sales									
32. Allocated Cost of Sales									
33. Allocated Operating Expenses									
34. Total Allocated									
35. Income (Loss) Before Tax									
36. INCOME AFTER TAX									
37. % Return on Sales									

C. AVERAGE ANNUAL INVESTMENT

							AVERAGE	AVERAGE	AVERAGE
38. Average Fixed Capital									
39. Average Proportionate Value of Existing Facilities to be Used									
40. Average Working Capital									
41. Average Cumulative Losses Before Tax (Exclusive of Depreciation)									
42. Total Average Annual Investment									

D. RETURN ON AVERAGE INVESTMENT
E. CASH POSITION END OF YEAR

105

The Use of Make-Buy to Reduce
a Price Increase

Appendix F

The Use of Make-Buy to Reduce a Price Increase

PM Corp. is a major industrial products manufacturer. One of its activities is the production of electrical and telephone equipment for aerospace transmission. PM purchases housings used in the manufacture of this equipment from a vendor—GAM, Inc. These housings, which will be called XYZ, are used to provide moisture and corrosive protection as well as mechanical strength. This case contains an interesting illustration of how the make-buy analysis was used by PM to reduce a proposed increase in the price of housings.

Background

The cost of XYZ housings had risen to about $1.10/unit including freight. The Aerospace Division of PM proposed that the housings be manufactured in-house. Led by Facilities Planning, the department responsible for capital expenditures, PM conducted a rather extensive XYZ housings make-or-buy study. This study will be illustrated in detail in this case.

The Long-Range Manufacturing Cost Summary on page 110 indicates that it would cost $4,081,200 to manufacture 5,095,000 housing units at a unit cost of $.801.

As the purchase price is $1.065/unit and freight is $.036/unit, the total cost to buy is $1.101/unit. Thus, the potential advantage to self-manufacturing is $.30/unit ($1.101 − $.801). At a volume of 5,095,000 housings, this represents an annual pre-tax savings of over $1.5 million.

In order to begin manufacturing, an investment of $1,039,600 would be required for new equipment. To determine the return of the proposal to self-manufacture and its effect on cash flows for the next 15 years, the detailed cash flow analysis presented on page 111 was prepared.

This statement estimates the effect of a decrease in purchases of XYZ housings and the increase in investment and expenses due to production. If these housings were manufactured in-house, cash flows would be increased by a total of $12,196,500 over this 15-year period.

XYZ Housings Production
Manufacturing Cost Summary
Long-Range Plan Average

	Manufacturing Cost	
	Total Cost	Cost Per Unit
Material		
Plasticizer	$2,899,200	.569
Plastic	387,200	.076
Freight to Plants	129,700	.025
	3,416,100	.670
Direct Labor and Fringes	75,800	.015
Indirect Labor, Salaries and Fringes	33,800	.007
Packaging Supplies	10,100	.002
Utilities	47,000	.009
Maintenance, Repairs and Supplies	21,000	.004
Waste	377,400	.074
Depreciation	100,000	.020
Total	$4,081,200	.801
Memo: Units	5,095,000	

According to the accompanying cash flow analysis, the pay-back period for the investment is 1.4 years. In addition, the net present value at 18%, the firm's cutoff rate, is $3,329, while the Discounted Cash Flow—ROI is 73.3%. This would therefore appear to be a very attractive investment indeed.

Alternatives

The above returns are based on the premise that there is a $.30/unit advantage to self-manufacture. If GAM, the supplier, reduces the price, however, the return would be diluted. In fact, the project return is extremely sensitive to the supplier's price of XYZ housings. Under the current view (a price of $1.065/unit) the project return would be 73.3%. If the price to PM Corp. would decrease more than $.25/unit, it was determined that the project's return would be less than the firm's 18% cutoff rate. Because return is so sensitive to the supplier's price, it was decided to investigate alternatives more closely before making a decision.

As the XYZ Housings Alternative Outcomes decision tree on page 112 indicates, PM could either negotiate with GAM for a price reduction or not.

XYZ HOUSINGS PRODUCTION
CASH FLOW ANALYSIS
(in 000's)

	0	1	2	3	4	5	6	7	8	9	10-14	15	Total
Investment													
Equipment	1,039.6												1,039.6
Inventory	235.0	31.0	25.0	10.0	(27.0)	-0-	-0-	-0-	-0-	-0-	-0-	(274.0)	-0-
Total	1,274.6	31.0	25.0	10.0	(27.0)	-0-	-0-	-0-	-0-	-0-	-0-	(274.0)	1,039.6
Costs													
Material Cost	-0-	(1,875.5)	(2,130.4)	(2,330.2)	(2,429.4)	(2,191.4)	(2,191.4)	(2,191.4)	(2,191.4)	(2,191.4)	(2,191.4)	(2,191.4)	(32,870.9)
D/L & Fringes	-0-	65.1	73.7	80.5	84.0	75.8	75.8	75.8	75.8	75.8	75.8	75.8	1,137.1
I/L & Fringes	-0-	29.0	32.8	35.9	37.4	33.8	33.8	33.8	33.8	33.8	33.8	33.8	506.9
Packaging Supplies	-0-	10.0	10.0	10.0	10.7	10.1	10.1	10.1	10.1	10.1	10.1	10.1	151.8
Utilities	-0-	40.3	45.7	49.9	52.1	47.0	47.0	47.0	47.0	47.0	47.0	47.0	705.0
Maintenance Rep. & Supp.	-0-	21.0	21.0	21.0	21.0	21.0	21.0	21.0	21.0	21.0	21.0	21.0	315.0
Waste	-0-	324.5	367.0	400.5	417.7	377.4	377.4	377.4	377.4	377.4	377.4	377.4	5,661.1
Depreciation	109.4	195.8	154.6	122.1	96.4	76.1	71.3	71.3	71.3	71.3	-0-	-0-	1,039.6
Pre-production Expense	100.0	-0-	-0-	-0-	-0-	-0-	-0-	-0-	-0-	-0-	-0-	-0-	100.0
Total	209.4	(1,189.8)	(1,425.6)	(1,610.3)	(1,710.1)	(1,550.2)	(1,555.0)	(1,555.0)	(1,555.0)	(1,555.0)	(1,626.3)	(1,626.3)	(23,254.4)
Cash Income													
Taxable Income	(209.4)	1,189.8	1,425.6	1,610.3	1,710.1	1,550.2	1,555.0	1,555.0	1,555.0	1,555.0	1,626.3	1,626.3	23,254.4
Tax (48%)	100.5	(571.1)	(684.3)	(772.9)	(820.8)	(744.1)	(746.4)	(746.4)	(746.4)	(746.4)	(780.6)	(780.6)	(11,161.9)
Depreciation	109.4	195.8	154.6	122.1	96.4	76.1	71.3	71.3	71.3	71.3	-0-	-0-	1,039.6
Investment Tax Credit (10%)	104.0	-0-	-0-	-0-	-0-	-0-	-0-	-0-	-0-	-0-	-0-	-0-	104.0
Cash Flow	(1,170.1)	783.5	870.9	947.5	1,014.7	882.2	879.9	879.9	879.9	879.9	845.7	1,119.7	12,196.5

Payback   1.4 years
NPV at 18% $3,329
DCF-ROI   73.3%

111

XYZ HOUSINGS ALTERNATIVE OUTCOMES

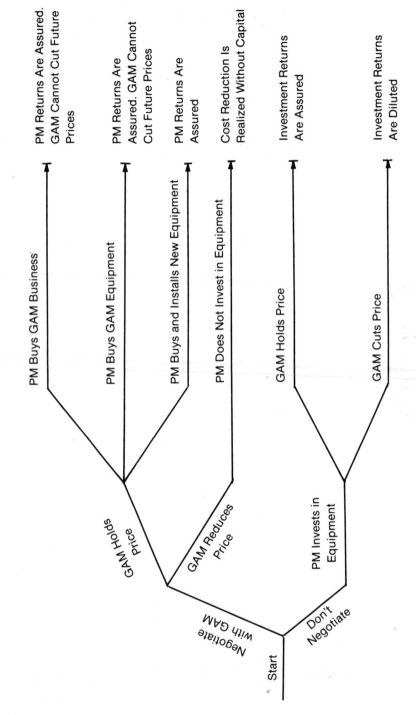

112

If PM *does not* negotiate, it will have to invest in the new equipment for manufacturing. Should GAM subsequently hold the price, PM's investment return is assured. If, however, GAM should reduce the price after PM is self-manufacturing the housings, the investment returns will be diluted. As indicated, if the price were cut by more than $.25, returns would be below the cutoff rate.

If the other alternative were followed and negotiations were held, GAM could either hold or reduce the price. The result of a sufficient price reduction would be that PM does not have to invest in new equipment yet will realize a cost reduction. On the other hand, if GAM holds the price, PM has three options. One is that it invests in the new equipment; since the price is being held, return on this investment would be assured for the present. The other two alternatives would be that PM could buy GAM's equipment or business that produces the housings. In each case, PM's return is further assured because GAM cannot cut future prices. The decision tree on page 112 was part of a report prepared by Facilities Planning. In it, the following recommendations were made:

Negotiating with GAM does not commit PM funds, and may result in a price reduction which could preclude the need for PM capital investment. The best alternative would be buying GAM's housings business or equipment at a reasonable price, since potential future price-cutting would be eliminated.

Negotiating with GAM is recommended, since it reduces uncertainty, as indicated on the attached sheet (decision tree). Purchasing concurs with this approach.

Prior to negotiating with GAM for a price reduction, Facilities Planning prepared a chart which attempted to quantify GAM's alternatives. The chart appears on page 114 and is based on these assumptions:

Assumptions
1. PM Average Usage = 5 million units
2. PM represents 40% of GAM's XYZ Sales
3. GAM makes $.30/unit profit on XYZ Sales

GAM can reduce the price to PM by an unknown amount — r. If this reduction is sufficient, PM would continue to purchase the housings from GAM rather than invest in new equipment for self-manufacture. This would result in GAM's losing $5 million r (PM's usage times the price reduction). This is alternative (D) on the chart.

On the other hand, if GAM holds the price, PM will invest and GAM then has three alternatives:

(A) It could reduce the price to the industry. This move would result in GAM's losing $1.5 million (the profit from PM's business—

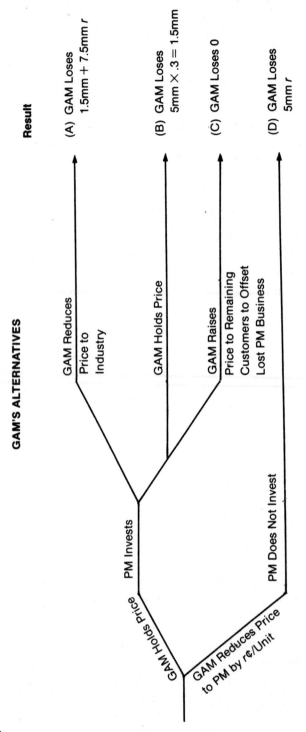

GAM'S ALTERNATIVES

Result

(A) GAM Loses
1.5mm + 7.5mm *r*

GAM Reduces
Price to
Industry

(B) GAM Loses
5mm × .3 = 1.5mm

GAM Holds Price

(C) GAM Loses 0

GAM Raises
Price to Remaining
Customers to Offset
Lost PM Business

(D) GAM Loses
5mm *r*

PM Invests

PM Does Not Invest

GAM Holds Price

GAM Reduces Price
to PM by *r*¢/Unit

$.30/unit $\times$ 5 million units) plus $7.5 million r (sales to others $\times$ the price reduction).

(B) It could hold the price to the remaining customers and lose only the profit from PM's business—$1.5 million.

(C) It could raise the price to the remaining customers to offset lost PM business. In this instance, GAM loses nothing.

Based on the above analysis, the following conclusions were drawn:

1. (C) is GAM's best alternative.
2. (D) is GAM's next best alternative for up to $.30/unit.
3. (A) plus (B) are always GAM's worst alternatives.

Although (C) would seem to be GAM's best alternative, this would be true only if it could raise prices to remaining customers to offset PM's lost business. At the current level of prices, it was determined that this was not feasible. Thus, it would seem that GAM's best alternative would be to reduce the price to PM rather than lose its business.

The Negotiations

Two meetings were held between PM and GAM, the supplier. The main participants were representatives from product and plant management, research, economic evaluation, and purchasing.

The fundamental issue raised by GAM at the meeting was the introduction of a new XYZ housing within the next three months. This new housing would use a different plastic and involve some modification to GAM's injection molding equipment. This modification would require a significant, though unspecified, investment by GAM.

Initially, this development caused a great deal of concern on the part of PM. Finally, it was agreed that this factor should not have an influence on PM's make-or-buy decision. First of all, it had not been established that the new housing would be superior to the old. Furthermore, it was estimated that since PM's equipment would be more flexible than that used by GAM, it could be modified to produce the new housing, if necessary, for about $100,000.

The remainder of the meetings were concerned with an analysis and critique of PM's estimated manufacturing costs. It was indicated that GAM felt PM would have to carry substantially more inventory than projected. It was further contended that PM's waste rates would be much higher, and it would have to employ additional engineering manpower on an ongoing basis to control this waste.

Although PM was not convinced that the supplier's assumptions were correct, the project returns were recalculated to reflect GAM's assertions. The following include the original and revised assumptions as they pertain to incremental finished goods inventory, engineering manpower and the waste rate.

Category	Original Assumption	Revised Assumption
Inventory	1 month raw materials—No incremental finished goods over plant inventories	1 month raw materials 2 months incremental finished over plant inventories
Manpower	No incremental engineering manpower	1 additional process engineer
Waste	15% waste rate	30% waste rate

Financial Impact

Assumption	DCF-ROI	Payback
Original	73.3%	1.4 years
Additional Inventory	49.2%	2.2 years
Additional Inventory, Manpower, Waste—Current XYZ Housing	37.6%	2.8 years
Additional Inventory, Manpower, Waste—Equipment Modified to Produce New XYZ Housing	36.2%	2.9 years

Assuming that additional finished goods inventory would have to be carried, the project would yield 49.2% instead of 73.3%. The impact of additional inventory, manpower, waste, and equipment modification would reduce the project return to 36.2%. Even with these assumptions, which are most probably highly pessimistic, the return remains attractive. Since no price concessions were granted, and GAM was unwilling to sell its housing business or equipment, it was decided that PM should go ahead with the investment in new equipment to manufacture XYZ housings.

Formal Action

Following is the complete package, sent to the Board of Directors of PM Corp., requesting approval to make the additional investment. It contains an excellent summary of this decision and is self-explanatory.

116

To the Board of Directors

The Aerospace Products Operation requests $1,040M capital for purchase and installation of XYZ housings manufacturing equipment. Associated working capital requirements total $235M.

XYZ housings are used as a protective covering in the manufacture of electrical and telephone equipment. Brill, Inc. developed XYZ with PM in the 1960's and has since specified its use.

GAM is PM's housing supplier. GAM holds patents covering XYZ housing supply. PM holds patents covering use of XYZ housing in electrical and telephone equipment and also has the right to self-manufacture. Price increases have brought the spread between anticipated in-house manufacturing costs and the purchase price to nearly $.30/unit.

Since PM uses 3-5MM housings annually, self-manufacture represents a $1.5MM savings possibility. This translates into a 70+% discounted cash flow rate of return. Expected payout would be less than two years. Negotiations with GAM have yielded negligible price concessions. Other alternatives to this request are unattractive.

Approval is requested to go forward with the XYZ manufacturing project.

Corporate Planning

Facilities Investment Commentary

DATE: January 26, 1977

AEROSPACE PRODUCTS OPERATION—

XYZ HOUSINGS MANUFACTURING FACILITIES: G-40 571-704

BACKGROUND: PM has a patent covering use of XYZ housings in electrical and telephone equipment manufacture. The plasticizer housing was developed jointly with Brill, Inc. Brill has specified that XYZ housing be used in this equipment since the mid-1960's to provide mechanical strength. R&D confirms that long-term continued use of XYZ is anticipated.

PM purchases its housings from GAM which has

117

a patent covering their supply. Prices have increased over $1/unit. PM purchases have recently averaged about $3MM/yr.

PROPOSED: Aerospace has proposed self-manufacture of XYZ housings. PM's patent permits manufacturing for in-house requirements. Estimated outlay would be $1,040M. Pre-tax savings of $1.5MM/yr. would be realized at anticipated volumes.

TECHNICAL
IMPLICATIONS: Requested funds cover purchase and installation of

• an injection molder	$450M
• flash remover	375
• packaging equipment	215
	$1,040M

Injection molding is the planned PM process. It is also used by GAM. Alternatives include film lamination and electrostatic coating. These latter process alternatives are not competitive because higher cost polyethylene is required as a base material.

PM has talked with equipment suppliers and GAM and has made housings on a pilot plant basis. A $100M pre-production start-up expense reflects a several-month learning curve.

A 15% premised scrap rate recognizes flashing loss as well as routine waste loss. No increased product waste is anticipated to be caused by housing self-manufacture.

LEGAL
IMPLICATIONS: PM legal and outside patent counsel have indicated that:

—PM can manufacture XYZ housings for its own use, and

—In doing so, they may employ film or plastic from GAM or others.

MARKETING STRATEGY:	This outlay does not alter Aerospace's electrical and telephone equipment marketing strategy except to provide a cost advantage over competition. No product price concessions are expected since Brill's housing prices are based on XYZ market price.

ECONOMICS: Attachment I shows that returns depend principally on the $.30/unit spread between PM costs and GAM's price. This spread yields a 73% expected DCF-ROR on a $1,275M investment base, including $235M in added inventory. Payout is less than two years.

SENSITIVITY: As seen from Attachment I, GAM's price would have to decline $.25/unit to cause this project to yield a marginal 18% return. Price is the key sensitivity factor. A 20% volume shift would only impact returns by 10%.

MATERIAL SOURCING: GAM has confirmed a willingness to sell PM plastic in lieu of housings. Should GAM's plastic price become unattractive, Hern plastic could be substituted.

ALTERNATIVES: Alternatives to this request have been identified and evaluated:

- Buy flash remover —shows lesser returns and limits sourcing,
- Buy GAM's XYZ equipment or business —GAM is unwilling to sell either,
- Buy housings from Tremp —Tremp's price equals GAM's,
- Negotiate a price reduction with GAM —this alternative has been pursued, to no avail. A last attempt will be made before implementing the project.

OTHER
FACTORS:

—GAM has indicated plans to introduce an improved housing. Should this occur, PM could duplicate it through equipment additions costing up to $125M.

—Wexlin's similar product has proved unsatisfactory.

—Excess flashing and injection capacity has alternate PM use.

COMMENTARY:

Product marketability, investment requirement, raw material and manufacturing costs are relatively firm. What causes this vertical integration decision to be difficult is GAM's unknown price reaction to losing up to 40% of its XYZ business. Should GAM maintain its price, or provide a • concession only to PM, PM would enjoy a margin advantage with or without investment. The only unfavorable outcome would be GAM's reducing price to the industry after PM invests.

BUDGET:

Aerospace's FEB includes funds for this project.

APPROVAL:

Approval of PM's Board of Directors is required.

RECOMMENDATION:

This request supports an important equipment business: commercial plastic equipment sales are planned at $60MM for 1977, yielding $7.4MM in gross profit.

While GAM's uncertain reaction jeopardizes returns, disapproval would eliminate expected savings exceeding $1.5MM/yr.

It is recommended that this project be approved, and that PM negotiate with GAM one last time before implementation.

_____   _____
Manager of Facilities Planning   Staff VP of Corporate Planning

ATTACHMENT I
UNIT COST COMPARISON
MAKE VS. BUY

($/unit of XYZ Housing)		MAKE	BUY
Finished XYZ Housing		—	1.065
Freight to Plants		.025	.036
Plasticizer @ $.665/lb., × 86%	=	.569	
Plastic @ $.53/lb. × 14%	=	.076	—
Direct Labor & Fringes		.015	—
Indirect Labor & Fringes		.007	—
Packaging Supplies		.002	—
Utilities		.009	—
Maintenance, Repair & Supplies		.004	—
Waste		.074	—
Depreciation		.020	—
		.801	$1.101

Advantage to self-manufacture = $1.101 − $.801 = $.30 = **$.30/unit**

PROJECT RETURN vs. GAM XYZ PRICE

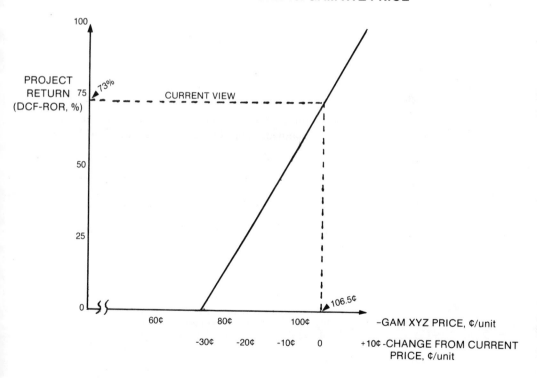

G-40 (7/69)

REQUEST FOR FIXED ASSET TRANSACTIONS
(In Thousands of U.S. Dollars)

ACQUISITION ☒
DISPOSAL ☐
TRANSFER ☐

(1) PROJECT TITLE	APPLICATION NO. 571-704	BUDGETED ☒
XYZ HOUSINGS PRODUCTION	AUTHORIZATION NO.	NON-BUDGETED ☐
	REFERENCE NO.	
	LOCATION HOUSTON	

(2) PROJECT REQUIREMENTS	AMOUNT AUTHORIZED ON PREV. REQ.	AMOUNT OF THIS REQUEST	TOTAL
LAND	–	–	–
BUILDINGS	–	–	–
EQUIPMENT	–	1,039.6	1,039.6
PROJECT RELATED EXPENSE			
TOTAL PROJECT	$ –	1,039.6	1,039.6

PLANNED STARTING DATE UPON APPROVAL PLANNED COMPLETION DATE 15 MONTHS AFTER COMPLETION

(3) FINANCIAL EVALUATION	FULL YEAR OF OPERATION					LONG-TERM AVERAGE	PAYOUT ON CAPITAL INVESTMENT
	YEAR 1	YEAR 2	YEAR 3	YEAR 4	YEAR 5		
Net Profit Before Taxes	$1233.6	$1528.2	$1680.2	$1754.5	$1574.3	$1574.3	
Return on Net Added Investment	60 %	65 %	73 %	79 %	76 %	103 %	1.4 YRS.

(4) EXPLANATION OF PURPOSE AND DESCRIPTION OF PROPOSAL (USE ADDITIONAL SHEET IF REQUIRED)

PROJECT SCOPE IS TO PRODUCE INTERNAL XYZ HOUSING NEEDS. DESIGN THROUGHPUT IS CONSISTENT WITH PRESENT PLANT CAPACITY.

THE METHOD OF PRODUCTION, INJECTION MOLDING WAS SELECTED BECAUSE OTHER ALTERNATIVES DID NOT SATISFY QUALITY OR PROJECT SCOPE CRITERIA.

1976 F.E.B. Item 11-A-1
MFP-149

(5) APPROVALS   PROJECT RESPONSIBILITY ASSIGNED TO _____

PLANT ACCOUNTANT DATE	OPERATIONS GEN. MGR. DATE	APPROPRIATIONS COMMITTEE DATE
PLANT MANAGER DATE	DATE	APPROPRIATIONS COMMITTEE DATE
OPERATIONS DIR. OF MFG./ SUBSIDIARY GENERAL MGR. DATE	DIRECTOR OF ENGINEERING DATE	APPROPRIATIONS COMMITTEE DATE
OPERATIONS CONTROLLER DATE	DATE	PRESIDENT – GCC DATE

Outcome

As recommended in the package to the Board of Directors, prior to implementation of the plan to manufacture, a final negotiation was held with the supplier. At this negotiation, the supplier granted a price reduction to PM. This confirmed the conclusion reached by PM that GAM would be better off reducing the price than losing its business. The price reduction was sufficient to mandate that PM continue to buy from GAM.

Bibliography

"A Formula for Make-or-Buy Decisions," *Purchasing Magazine,* September 19, 1972, pp. 85-87.

Beckmann, Neal W., "Purchasing's New Role in the Make or Buy Decision," *St. Louis Purchaser,* January 1975, pp. 64-67, 70.

Burton, Richard M., and H. Peter Holzer, "To Make or Buy?", *Management Services,* July-August 1968, pp. 26-31.

_____ and D. J. Laughhunn, "On the Optimality of Single-Item, Incremental Cost Rules for the Make-Buy Decision," *The Engineering Economist,* Summer 1971, pp. 227-246.

Brinkeroff, James F., "The Decision to Make or Purchase," in *Operations Research Applied: New Uses and Extensions,* Special Report No. 17, American Management Association, New York, 1957, pp. 109-118.

Caditz, Clement C., "Make or Buy: Some Facts and Fallacies," in *Purchasing for Profit: Practical Guides for Cost Reduction,* Management Report No. 20, American Management Association, New York, 1958, pp. 53-57.

Cochran, E. B., "The Special Importance of the 'Make or Buy' Decision—With Some Suggestions for Sharper Analysis," in *Modern Approaches to Production Planning and Control,* (Robert A. Pritzker and Robert A. Gring, eds.) American Management Association, New York, 1960, pp. 213-236.

Culliton, James W., *Make or Buy,* Harvard University Division of Business Research, Boston, Mass., 1961.

Dixon, Robert L., "Some Economic Considerations in Make-or-Buy Decisions," *Home Appliance Builder,* January 1966, pp. 17-20.

Doney, Lloyd D., "Coping with Uncertainty in the Make or Buy Decision," *Management Accounting,* October 1968, pp. 31-34.

Dowst, Somerby, "Make or Buy: Delivery Problems Can Tip the Scales," *Purchasing,* September 21, 1976, pp. 47, 49, 51.

Duncan, Ian D., "Make-or-Buy Decisions," *Cost and Management,* September-October 1975, pp. 44-49.

Dusinberre, Peter De K., Jr., "The 'Make or Buy' Decision as a Factor in Manufacturing Costs," in *The Manufacturing Man and His Job* (Robert E.

Finley and Henry R. Ziobro, eds.), American Management Association, New York, 1966, pp. 386-395.

England, Wilbur B. and Michael R. Leenders, *Purchasing and Materials Management* (Chapter 12: Procurement by Manufacture), Dow Jones-Irwin, Homewood, Ill., 1975, pp. 771-793.

Gordon, Lawrence A., Danny Miller, and Henry Mintzberg, *Normative Models in Managerial Decision-Making,* National Association of Accountants, New York, and The Society of Management Accountants of Canada, Ontario, Canada, 1975.

Gross, Harry, *Make or Buy,* Prentice-Hall, Inc., Englewood Cliffs, N.J., 1966.

_____ "Make or Buy Decisions in Growing Firms," *The Accounting Review,* October 1960, pp. 745-753.

_____ "Purchasing Procedures for Make or Buy Decisions," *Journal of Purchasing,* November 1966, pp. 63-73.

Hackamack, Lawrence C., *Should You Make or Buy Components?,* Small Business Administration Management Aids No. 189, Washington, D.C., June 1967.

Higgins, Carter C., "Make-or-Buy Re-Examined," *Harvard Business Review,* March-April 1955, pp. 109-119.

_____ "You Can Form Rational Make-or-Buy Decisions," *American Business,* February 1959, pp. 36-37.

Hubler, Myron J., Jr., "Make or Buy Decisions," in *Financial Executives Handbook* (R.F. Vancil, ed.), Dow Jones-Irwin, Homewood, Ill., 1970, pp. 288-303.

_____ "The Make or Buy Decisions," *Management Services,* November-December 1966, pp. 45-51.

Klawson, Rennold L., "Packager's Decision: Make or Buy?" *Management Review,* October 1965, pp. 57-61.

Lee, Lamar, Jr., and Donald W. Dobler, *Purchasing and Materials Management: Text and Cases* (Chapter 15: Make or Buy), McGraw-Hill Book Co., New York, 1977, pp. 301-316.

Leibson, I., and C. A. Trischman, Jr., "Should You Make or Buy Your Major Raw Materials?", *Chemical Engineering,* February 21, 1972, pp. 76-84.

Levey, Gary D. "The Second Aim," *Management Accounting,* June 1974, pp. 47-49.

Lopez, A. W., "Make Or Buy!", *Chemical Purchasing,* May 1976, pp. 15-18.

Madison, Jim, "The 'Make or Buy' Decision," *Management Accounting,* February 1973, pp. 32-34.

"Make or Buy Decisions," *Management Accounting* (English), November 1967, pp. 465-468.

"Make or Buy Is Many-Sided," *Purchasing,* September 3, 1974, pp. 51, 53.

"Management Services Forum," *Management Services,* July-August 1970, pp. 1-3.

"Manufacturing Policy: The Make-or-Buy Decision," *The CPA Journal,* June 1972, pp. 492-493.

McConeghy, George C., "Data for Make-or-Buy Decisions," in *Reporting Financial Data to Top Management,* Special Report No. 25, American Management Association, New York, 1957, pp. 94-98.

Mitchell, Gibson E., "The Make-or-Buy Decision—A Case Study," *Management Accounting,* November 1967, pp. 41-5.

Mock, Edward J., and David F. Miller, "The 'Make or Buy' Decision Under Uncertainty," *Journal of Systems Management,* May 1970, pp. 13-17.

National Association of Accountants, *Statements on Management Accounting Practices: Criteria for Make-or-Buy Decisions,* Statement No. 5, Author, New York, June 21, 1973.

National Association of Purchasing Management, *Make or Buy,* No. 38, Leaders Guide, Author, New York, 1972.

Oxenfeldt, A. R., and M. W. Watkins, *Make or Buy,* McGraw-Hill Book Co., New York, 1956.

Paton, William A., "Make-or-Buy Decisions—Factors and Measurements," *Michigan Business Review,* March 1966, pp. 7-13.

Paton, William A., and Robert L. Dixon, *Make-or-Buy Decision in Tooling for Mass Production,* Michigan Business Reports, No. 35, Bureau of Business Research, School of Business Administration, The University of Michigan, Ann Arbor, Mich., 1961.

"Purchasing Role in Cost Reduction," *The Accountant,* August 9, 1973, pp. 180-181.

Raunick, Donald A., and Armen G. Fisher, "A Probabilistic Make-Buy Model," *Journal of Purchasing,* February 1972, pp. 63-80.

Reilly, Edward C., "Make-or-Buy: Is Do It Yourself the Solution?", *Northwest Business Management,* Fall 1966, pp. 27-29.

Roe, P. A., "Modelling a Make or Buy Decision at ICI," *Long Range Planning,* December 1972, pp. 21-26.

Rosen, Robert W., "Least Cost vs. Opportunity Cost in Make or Buy Decisions," *Financial Executive,* January 1966, pp. 40-43.

Schuba, Kenneth F., "Make-or-Buy Decisions—Costs and Non-Cost Considerations," *NAA Bulletin,* March 1960, pp. 53-66.

Shore, Barry, "Quantitative Analysis and the Make-or-Buy Decision,"*Journal of Purchasing,* February 1970, pp. 5-11.

Teresko, John, "Make or Buy? New Issues Force the Decisions," *Industry Week,* September 4, 1978, pp. 34-37.

"To Make or Buy—It's More Than A Question of Economy," *Accountants Weekly*, April 28, 1978, pp. 20-21.

Ward, Edwin F., "Making the Proper Make-or-Buy Decision," *NAA Bulletin*, January 1964, pp. 31-32.

Westing, J. H., I.V. Fine, Gary Joseph Zenz, *Purchasing Management: Materials in Motion* (Chapter 13: Make or Buy), John Wiley & Sons, Inc., New York 1976, pp. 275-291.

Wulff, Peter, "Make-or-Buy Decisions Shift Like Quicksand," *Purchasing Magazine*, September 19, 1972, pp. 83-85.

_____, "Make-or-Buy: Teamwork Pays Off," *Purchasing Magazine*, December 25, 1969, pp. 27, 28, 30, 31.

No. 80120-GP-2.5M-11/80